CONVERSATIONS IN

The Garden of Shizen

自然

*Jesus of the
Gospels, women, sex
and the family*

D W PHILLIPS

For Tom, Tooney, and Emily
for their help and encouragement,
and for Jane
valgami lo lungo studio e il grande amore

ISBN 1 903816 10 6

Write to: John Hunt Publishing Ltd,
46A West Street, Alresford,
Hampshire SO24 9AU, UK

Printed in Guernsey, Channel Islands.

Visit us on the Web at: www.o-books.net

CONVERSATIONS IN

The Garden
of Shizen

自然

*Jesus of the
Gospels, women, sex
and the family*

D W PHILLIPS

BOOKS

Contents

Acknowledgements

A number of contemporary authors are quoted in the conversations, and all the quotations are fully referenced in the Notes and References section of the book. While writing this book, the author has constantly consulted the *New Jerusalem Bible*, published and copyright 1985 by Darton, Longman and Todd Ltd and Doubleday & Co Inc, and the quotations from the notes to that translation are made by permission of the publishers.

The author would also like to thank the following publishers, who have given permission to quote from books published by them: Blackwell Publishers Ltd, Cambridge University Press, Continuum Publishing, Peter Halban Publishers, HarperCollins Publishers, New Directions Publishing Corporation, Other Press (publishers of *The Psychoanalytic Quarterly*), Oxford University Press, Penguin Books Ltd, Random House, Inc (Alfred A. Knopf Inc: present copyright holders of *The sailor who fell from grace with the sea*, by Yukio Mishima, translated by John Nathan), SCM Press, Thames & Hudson Ltd, and Weidenfeld & Nicolson.

While every reasonable effort has been made to trace all the owners of copyright of the books quoted, in a very few cases this has regrettably not proved possible.

The author would particularly like to thank Teriko Sekiguchi, librarian at the Japan Information and Cultural Centre, London W1, for the reference to the folk-tale of Shima no Ko, and Hiroko Takamoto for verifying the occasional utterances in Japanese that appear in the text. Thanks, finally, to John Hunt and to Anne O'Rorke, his managing editor, and to Anne Gowan, who introduced the author to his publisher.

Introduction

Should priests be celibate? Should there be women priests? Should active homosexuals be allowed to be clergymen? Should homosexual marriages be allowed? Should a divorced person be allowed a church marriage? Are there sexual sins that will be punished by everlasting fire in hell?

If the press and the broadcasting media are anything to go by, these are the questions that agitate a Christendom that in earlier times quarrelled bitterly over the essential nature of Jesus of Nazareth, and divided doctrinally, at least, into two major sects, the eastern Orthodox and the western Catholic, over the exact provenance of the Holy Spirit.

The Gospels of the New Testament — the four Gospels recognised by the Christian churches and known for that reason as canonical — tell us all we really know about Jesus, but they are far from being historical documents. Apart from having been compiled a generation or more after Jesus' death, they constitute a literary genre of their own, inextricably mixing theological interpretation with what purport to be records of the actual words and deeds of Jesus. The first three Gospels — Mark, the earliest to be written, Matthew and Luke — are known to biblical scholars as the synoptic Gospels, because the similarity between them in subject matter and order of presentation allows them to be set out visually for comparison one with the others. The fourth Gospel, however, traditionally attributed to John, was probably written later than the other three, and differs significantly from them in both style and content. Most importantly, it has a far more developed exposition of the divine status of Jesus.

Christianity has come a long way since Christ, and this process probably began during his own lifetime, when he was already a legend. And if Jesus of Nazareth were to return as a man to the world today, he would be baffled by much Christian doctrine and shocked by much Christian practice. But what would disconcert him most would be to find the sublunary world still in existence, because while he was on earth in the first century, he fully expected this world to come to an end at any minute. According to the Gospels, he prophesied the end of the world and his glorious return in the clouds in the lifetime of some of those who were present when he made this prophecy. The failure of this prophecy to be fulfilled was an embarrassment to the generation that succeeded Jesus, and if they had invented this prophecy, they would simply have been contriving their own lack of credibility. It follows that the prophecy is one that Jesus certainly uttered.

But how much of what Jesus is reported as saying and doing in the Gospels he actually said and did is far from certain, and the many attempts to retrieve the so-called historical Jesus from the

Gospels have been unsuccessful. It may be safer to assert what he did not say or do. So, to return to present-day preoccupations, he said nothing, for instance, about women priests, and for that matter, made only two or three references to men priests.

The Christians invented a new word for 'priest' — *presbuteros* (literally, 'an older man'). But Jesus did not use this word, from which the English word 'priest' ultimately derives. Nor was the word *episkopos* ('overseer' — the origin of the word 'bishop') in Jesus' vocabulary.

The Christian male priesthood is supposed to depend on unbroken succession from Jesus' male disciples, his many female followers being excluded by most Christian churches from this continuum. But in view of Jesus' belief in the imminent destruction of the world, it is difficult to figure out how he could have wanted to authorise a succession of this kind, continuing through dozens of subsequent generations of mankind.

There are other modern preoccupations on which Jesus said nothing explicit, while on some specifically sexual matters he had — according to the Gospels — quite a lot to say, more often than not of an uncomfortable severity. These are the questions explored in these conversations between William Whitland, a layman and an amateur student of the Gospels, and two Japanese anthropologists. They start from the assumption that, however unreliable the Gospels may be as a historical account of Jesus' teaching, and however far the various Christian churches have advanced since Jesus' day, the Jesus of the Gospels still presents the main mystery and the main challenge to believers and non-believers in Christianity alike.

The book has been put together from the transcripts of conversations held mostly in the university garden between William Whitland and Shoji Kamada, professor of the anthropology of religion at Dokokani University, and his assistant, Dr Masako Hiraoka. Professor Kamada studied at American universities for five years and, in editing the transcripts, I have tried to retain his original words as much as possible. I have, however, made a few corrections to his English, and more to Dr Hiraoka's in the interests of making what they have to say easier reading, without, I hope, at all altering the sense they intend. The notes and references have been compiled from manuscript notes made by Whitland, and from a number of books he has put at my disposal, which he has marked with underlining and with marginal notes.

Throughout the conversations, Whitland has made his own translations from the original Greek of the Gospels. This he did partly to avoid any problems with copyright, but also to show that the Greek is often more down-to-earth and in a more naive narrative style than the established translators care to show. At the same time, however, Whitland has checked his translation against other versions, which he appears to know by heart.

Chapter 1

☙

Procreation without sex

Whitland I came down here yesterday towards dusk, and I thought, as I listened to the water splashing over the rocks and sniffed the scent of the wild carnations and roses, that art alone could not design a garden as beautiful as this, and neither could nature. It is only when these two come together that such an atmosphere can be created.

Kamada Yes. The Japanese garden has always been nature designed by man — nature as art. It has been said, too, that our gardens express the essence of our country. There is a special association with Buddhism, of course, but aren't gardens important in Christianity, as well?

Whitland It has never struck me.

Kamada But in your holy scriptures, aren't the first human pair brought to life in a garden?

Whitland Yes, when God has created Adam, the first man, out of the dust of the ground, he takes him and puts him in the garden of Eden, to cultivate it and look after it. It's all in the Book of Genesis — a Greek word that means 'coming into being'.

Kamada And the first woman? Are you forgetting her?

Whitland She came later. God put Adam into a deep sleep, and while he was asleep took out one of his ribs and made it into a helpmate for him, apparently a fully formed adult, our ancestress Eve. So the first woman was born from a man, instead of the usual way, which is the other way round. But this doesn't mean that Adam played an active part here: he is, according to one modern commentator who apparently finds some kind of truth in the story, 'not participant, not even onlooker at the divine activity which builds a rib into a woman'.

Kamada So who was the witness of God's activity? Who was there to see Eve fashioned in this way, and to record the event?

Whitland No one, as far as I know. But it's not a piece of history, after all, but a myth — a figment of the human imagination, if you like, but one that tries to answer a riddle: how did the first human beings appear on earth?

Kamada Of course! Yet there are still some people who take the story literally. But we have equally imaginative myths about the origin of our Japanese ancestors, and I suppose that stories of this kind are found all over the world. It's obvious, too, that the primeval pair cannot themselves be accounted for by the sexual act, for that would lead simply to an earlier pair, still calling for explanation. So, in one Egyptian myth, for example, you have Khnemu, the potter god, giving form to man on his potter's wheel. And in Babylon, one of the gods mixes blood and soil to create human beings.

Whitland Most of these myths come in a number of versions. In fact, it's usually impossible to get a story out of them that hangs together in its details, even if you take the myths on their own terms. But that's not so surprising, when you think that all these myths originated before writing of any kind — they're prehistoric, in other words.

Kamada Yes, but there is something that impresses me here. Let us allow that the Book of Genesis is myth, rather than history. It is to be found in the sacred scriptures of the ancient people of Israel, isn't it?

Whitland Yes, it is the first book in what Jews call the *Tanakh*, and is known to Christians as the Old Testament. That's a collection of books that tell the story of the ancient Jews — but in such a way as to present them as a people specially chosen by God to establish his reign of justice on earth. But I believe you are more interested in the books that form the second half of the Christian Bible and establish the foundation of Christian belief — I mean the New Testament.

Kamada Yes, and that is why Dr Hiraoka suggested I should get in touch with you. She said your own research may in some ways run parallel to ours.

Whitland She is too kind. I honestly cannot call my miscellaneous reading 'research'. With your indulgence, I must insist on my amateur status!

Kamada But you have studied these sacred writings, I am sure. And you read them in their original language, Greek.

Whitland Yes, that's true.

Kamada I have been to Greece twice, and I have visited so many of their churches and temples! But Jesus was not a Greek, and it is strange that the New Testament was written in Greek.

Whitland It was the international language of the day. At least, it was in the eastern Mediterranean. Jesus himself may perhaps have known some Greek, because many of the country-folk in Galilee, the province of Israel where he spent his childhood, were bilingual in Greek and Aramaic. But Jesus' first language was certainly Aramaic, a language related to Hebrew. Perhaps he's the only great spiritual teacher whose original words — I mean the words of his own language — are almost completely lost to us. But you were saying that something especially impressed you.

Kamada Ah, yes! We agreed, I believe, that the various creation myths known to us all date from prehistoric times. But the New Testament is not prehistoric, is it?

Whitland Certainly not! In fact, Christians make a big thing of the fact that their religion is rooted in specific historical events.

Kamada But here is what impressed me. A strange thing about your Bible is this: the first part of it, the Hebrew sacred scriptures, begins by denying the woman's role in the creation of an offspring; and the second part, devoted to the Christian message, begins by denying the man's.

Whitland You mean...

Kamada I have read this New Testament, you see. And I am referring to the story in the first book, you know...

Whitland The book we call the Gospel according to Saint Matthew?

Kamada Yes, that is the book. It begins with the story of the birth of Jesus, whose father, it says, had no part in his conception. So I have to ask myself, isn't this a myth, but, in view of what we've been saying, not a myth in the usual prehistoric mode? To put my question another way, is Jesus, in spite of being a historical figure, also a mythical one? This is a difficult problem for me.

Whitland Perhaps Jesus is a mythical figure — the last myth in the Western world. Right up to modern times we've had legendary figures — there are people who insist that Che Guevara, the Argentinean guerrilla leader, is still alive, or will come back to life, and there's a widespread cult of the American rock musician, Elvis Presley. But neither of these has the slightest makings of a myth properly so-called.

Kamada You are making a distinction here between legend and myth.

Whitland Yes. To my mind, there are several important differences between them. A myth condenses the truth, while a legend expands it. And the essential purpose of a myth is to explain something — usually the origin of some phenomenon or set of phenomena. I'm not sure whether a legend, on the other hand, has a purpose at all — not a conscious one, anyway. But it does obviously answer a need — perhaps to console people, or to give them something to identify with.

But to return to Matthew's account of the conception and birth of Jesus, many people have a problem with it, even if they don't express it in quite the way that you have done. They are troubled not so much by the conflict between myth and history that you have remarked as by the whole possibility of virgin birth. Some people have even looked at instances of this phenomenon among insects and flowers, to see if they can accommodate the story in Matthew.

May I mention one particular difficulty I have myself? It is this: in keeping with some general biblical ideas on the subject, the New Testament — Matthew's Gospel, that is — begins with a list of Jesus' male ancestors — 42 of them — linking his father Joseph in a direct line to Abraham, the founder of the Hebrew people. Only four women are mentioned in this list, apparently because they were foreigners.

But having gone to all that trouble to ferret out Joseph's descent from Abraham, the author of that opening Gospel about Jesus, Matthew, goes on to explain that Joseph, after all, was not Jesus' father — he had nothing to do with the conception of Jesus.

Matthew puts it in these words: 'Jacob was the father of Joseph, the husband of Mary, of whom Jesus, called the Anointed, was born. Now the birth of Jesus the Anointed was like this: his mother Mary was engaged to be married to Joseph, but before they lived together she was found to be pregnant by the Holy Spirit.'

Kamada The Holy Spirit? This is the same as God, the Christian God, isn't it?

Whitland You will have to ask a Christian theologian to explain the Holy Spirit to you, I'm afraid. Matthew, however, was writing his book about Jesus three hundred years before the Christian Church worked out a fully formulated account of a God who is at the same time three in one and one in three: God the Father, God the Son, and God the Holy Spirit.

Matthew was a Jew, apparently writing for Jews, and the Jewish idea of the Holy Spirit was that it was the breath of God, the means by which he created life. There is no notion there of the Holy Spirit as a separate person, as it is in Christian belief. So I am not at all qualified to say exactly what Matthew understood by the Holy Spirit.

Of course, some Christians have had a big problem with this three-person God, Isaac Newton and Leo Tolstoy among them, if I remember rightly. But isn't there also a Holy Trinity in Buddhism?

Kamada You are thinking, perhaps, of the Three-body Doctrine of the Great Vehicle School — we call it the Daijo School here in Japan — according to which the Buddha appears under three different aspects, or at three distinct levels.

Whitland Yes. In my own mind, I think of them as earthly, heavenly, and — I was going to say metaphysical Buddhas. The last aspect, or body is somehow identified with absolute truth, and is said also to symbolise the inner unity of all three Buddha manifestations. So here again, there seems to be a notion of three in one and one in three.

Kamada But the Buddha is not God! The Enlightened one — the Butsu we call him — had no belief in God nor in anything properly called divine.

Whitland But in any case, I don't suppose for one minute, do you, that one can arrive at a full understanding of these questions by pursuing a merely logical path.

Kamada If you are referring to some kind of direct experience, to something mystical or beyond ordinary experience, or at least to something that lies beyond description, then I think there is an opposition between that and what you call theology. Perhaps that is a typically Japanese view!

Whitland Let us leave it there for the moment, *Kamada-sama*! We shall have many other opportunities to meet and talk about these matters, as often as possible, I hope, in this delightful garden.

Kamada Thank you very much indeed.

Chapter 2

Jesus and his heavenly Father

Kamada When I read the Gospels not in their biblical order, but in the order in which they were written, beginning with Mark and ending with John, I formed the impression that, as far as Jesus' relation with God went, there was a progression. At the beginning he is distinct from God. At the end he is one with God. Have I understood correctly?

Whitland As usual with the Gospels, the question is a complex one, but there is undoubtedly something in what you say.

Kamada Mark's Gospel is usually taken to have been written before the others, and Matthew and Luke draw on his account to some extent. That's true, isn't it?

Whitland It's certainly the general view, and I gather that even Roman Catholic scholars, or many of them, now accept it.

Kamada Very early in Mark, Jesus undergoes a ritual of purification in the waters of the River Jordan, and a voice from the sky — the voice of God — hails him as 'my Son, my beloved.' Immediately after that, we are told that the Spirit sent him away into the desert, to be tested by Satan. Mark does not say who Satan is — he evidently expects his readers to know. But I gather that Satan is a person, also known as the Devil, and he is God's main enemy.

Whitland Yes, that's right.

Kamada And the Spirit?

Whitland Mark means God, I'm sure.

Kamada Mark's account of this incident is very short, almost perfunctory in view of its strangeness: that God orders this test for his Son. Even stranger is Matthew's elaboration of the story. There the Devil challenges Jesus as Son of God, and Jesus rebukes him with a quotation from the ancient Jewish scriptures: 'You will not put your Lord God to the test!' Isn't all this very strange?

Whitland To a modern mind, yes. But in the context of what people believed at the time...

Kamada But it is even stranger in that context. Because if Jesus was the Son of God, and indeed was one of the three persons making up the three-in-one, one-in-three God — the Holy Trinity of Christian belief — here is God contriving his own test by the Devil. Look at it, if I may so put it, from God's point of view: what is to be gained?

Whitland I can hardly do that — look at it from God's point of view, I mean. But I can say this: although Matthew insists that Jesus is the Son of God, with a unique knowledge of God, he nowhere says Jesus was God. And in the desert, not even the Devil calls Jesus *the* son of God, but only says to him: 'If you are Son of God.' That could mean 'a son of God'. There's a difference here in Greek as well as in English.

Kamada But not in Japanese! Again I should like to ask who witnessed this test in the desert. Jesus was alone, wasn't he?

Whitland Yes, according to the Gospels no one else was there... except the Devil!

Kamada Then I suppose we must simply assume that Jesus told his pupils about it himself.

Whitland His disciples, yes.

Kamada So we have God devising this test for himself, passing the test, and then telling the disciples in all seriousness about it.

Whitland Well, if you put it like that... But in defence of Matthew, perhaps he had no clear idea that Jesus was one of the persons of the three-person God.

Kamada So where did this idea, that Jesus in some way actually was God, arise?

Whitland You mentioned just now Mark's report that a voice was heard from the sky, when Jesus was baptised. Although Mark does not say so, we have to assume it was God's voice, and he calls Jesus 'My son, the one I love.' That seems to be the earliest statement of a particular relationship between Jesus and God.

Soon after that, Mark tells us about some demons that Jesus has exorcised from sick people. These impure spirits, as Mark calls them, shout at Jesus: 'You are the Son of God!'

I take it that the implication is that spirits — even impure ones — are quicker to recognise him as a spiritual being than men and women in the non-spiritual world are. Jesus then tells these spirits not to make him known — he means, not to publicise the fact that he is the Son of God.

In Mark's Gospel, it is only when Jesus is interrogated by the Jewish High Priest that he claims outright, explicitly and unambiguously, to be the anointed one, the awaited King of the Jews sent by God to liberate them, the Son of the Blessed One, whom the chief priests and other dignitaries assembled in the High Priest's house will see 'sitting on the right hand of power'.

Kamada But Jesus does not say in as many words that he is God?

Whitland Not in Mark. And at one point he explicitly distinguishes himself from God — really denies the suggestion that he is God. This is when a rich young man addresses Jesus as 'Good Master', and Jesus replies: 'Why do you call me good? No one is good, except God alone.'

Luke confirms that Jesus is *the* Son of God, and he is the only Gospel writer to tell the story of the twelve-year-old Jesus making an implicit claim to this status when speaking to his earthly father, Joseph — his first manifestation of his consciousness of being 'the Son', as some modern scholars point out.

Luke is also alone in having Jesus tell his disciples that he confers royalty upon them, 'just as my Father conferred it on me,' but nowhere does Luke claim that Jesus is God.

In fact, it is only in John's Gospel, probably written sixty or seventy years after Jesus' death, and a generation after the other three Gospels, that Jesus is identified with God.

John not only states most clearly that Jesus is *the* Son of God, and indeed the only Son of God, but he reports Jesus himself claiming that the Father loves the Son; that the Father has sent him; that only the Son has seen the Father; that the Father glorifies him; and that he knows the Father.

But most astonishing of all is Jesus' declaration: 'I and the Father are one.' According to the theologians, this statement by Jesus is 'deliberately undefined and hints at a more comprehensive and a profounder unity', or 'is clearly meant to refer to a unity in eternal being.' I cannot claim that I understand what they mean by these remarks, which strike me as prime examples of what the German philosopher Joachim Kahl has identified as a structural principle of Christian theology — the striving after what he calls 'maximum content'.

Kamada You did say, 'I and the Father'? Not even, 'the Father and I'?

Whitland Yes, but that was simply the usual way of putting things in the Greek of that time.

Kamada But if Jesus really did utter these words, and they are not, so to speak, merely a Greek invention, isn't it even more astonishing that the earlier Gospels do not report them?

Whitland Well, it has to be said that the Jesus portrayed by John is very different from the Jesus of the other narratives, and the great twentieth-century German interpreter of the New Testament, Rudolf Bultmann, even declares that the Gospel of John cannot be taken into account at all as a source for the teaching of Jesus.

You're right, too, to be impressed by the word 'I' — *ego* in Greek — in this statement. This exemplifies one of the most glaring differences between John and the earlier Gospels.

In Greek, the personal pronoun *ego* is not needed and is not often used with the verb in the first person: the form of the verb shows who is speaking. So *ego* is a rare word in Mark's Gospel, and he puts it into Jesus' mouth only nine or ten times. But in John's Gospel, Jesus utters the word 120 or so times. And the sort of things he says about himself usually have no obvious parallel in the other Gospels.

Chapter 3

⌒

Jesus and his earthly father

Kamada We talked about Jesus' relation to God, his Father in the sky, the other day, but is there nothing to be gathered from the Gospels about his earthly father, Joseph?

Whitland Not a great deal, I think. Mark makes no mention at all of Joseph, and he fails to describe any of the remarkable events attending the birth of Jesus that are reported by Matthew and Luke.

In John's Gospel, there are two brief references to Joseph: one when Philip, one of Jesus' newly-recruited disciples, tells his friend Nathanael that he has found the man that Moses and the prophets wrote about, namely 'Jesus son of Joseph, from Nazareth'; and the second, when the Jews murmur disapprovingly, 'Surely, this is Jesus son of Joseph; we know his father and mother.' and they ask how can he now say, 'I have come down from heaven.'

Kamada Is that all that the Gospels say?

Whitland No, there is more about Joseph in Matthew and Luke. According to Matthew, when Joseph found out that Mary was expecting a baby before they had slept together, his first intention was to divorce her secretly, but he changed his mind after a dream. In this dream, one of God's messengers told him what had happened, and that he was to marry Mary, and call the son she would give birth to

'Jehoshua', a name meaning in Hebrew 'God saves'. 'Jesus' is the Greek form of the name.

Joseph acted as the messenger told him, but did not sleep with Mary (so Matthew says) until the time when she gave birth to a son.

Joseph has another dream in the second chapter of Matthew, when God's messenger warns him to take his wife and baby son to Egypt to frustrate King Herod's plan to murder the child. Later, after Herod's death, the angel appeared to Joseph in yet another dream, and told him to take the child and his mother back to Israel. This episode, known as 'the flight into Egypt' is not mentioned by the other Gospel writers, and certainly owes a lot to various Old Testament prophecies.

Kamada He seems to have been something of a dreamer, this Joseph!

Whitland Pious Christians would say this was God's way of making his commands known to a simple man.

Kamada But he was a carpenter, wasn't he? I'm sure I've read that somewhere.

Whitland That's also in Matthew, where some people in a synagogue — a building set aside by the Jews for worship and the study of the sacred scriptures — express their amazement at hearing Jesus talk, and ask, 'Isn't he the carpenter's son?'

Some people have said that the Greek word *tekton* used here means something a bit higher in the social scale, a kind of master craftsman, say. I myself find it interesting that in his great cosmological dialogue, the *Timaeus*, Plato talks about the maker and father of 'this everything', and asks 'what did the contriver of it use as a model?' — and the 'contriver' is the *tektainomenos* in Plato's Greek, a word from the same root as *tekton*. The English word 'architect' is also related, of course.

And by the way, Plato's notion that 'this everything', this universe, is the result of deliberate construction on the part of a creator God was new to Greek thought, but you can see that it is close to the account in the Book of Genesis.

Kamada But quite foreign to any Buddhist notions.

Whitland But I'm losing track of what I wanted to say. You see, I have sometimes wondered whether the belief that Jesus was the son of a *tekton* and, indeed, a *tekton* himself, does not incorporate some symbolic, even mythical significance.

Kamada It may be so. But you still have not told me about Luke's account of Joseph.

Whitland Luke mentions Joseph briefly in his nativity narrative, and even calls him Jesus' father, without any qualification, when Jesus is presented in the Temple shortly after his birth. But when Luke introduces his version of Jesus' ancestry, which he does at the beginning of Jesus' ministry, he seems aware of the anomaly of tracing it back through Joseph, and says, in a rather lame parenthesis, that Jesus 'was thought' to be the son of Joseph. Some scholars justify these long genealogies in Matthew and Luke by saying that they establish Jesus' legal claim to belong to the house of the tenth-century BC king of Israel, David.

Luke also refers to Joseph, though not by name, in the story of the twelve-year-old Jesus in the Temple, that we have already talked about. The brief answer that Jesus is supposed to have given his parents on that occasion implicitly repudiated any notion that Joseph might be entitled to be called his father, and at the same time laid claim to a special relationship with God. This is the first mention in Luke of 'my father', meaning God, and whether this was Luke's intention or not,

Jesus' words here create the impression that it was he himself who, as a child not yet in his teens, denied his earthly father, and adopted a heavenly one.

Now, except for one brief, passing reference, there is no other mention of Joseph in Luke's Gospel.

Kamada The story of Joseph is a strange one from this point of view: his role is altogether superfluous, unless one accepts the notion that he was needed, for legal reasons so to speak, to establish Jesus' link with the royal house. What I mean is that in most traditions of this kind, of the earthly incarnation of a deity — what is called *avatara* in Hinduism — there is no human agent involved, not even one who, like poor Joseph, is brought into the drama only to be denied a speaking part. Of course, if one looks at the whole story as a purely human contrivance, one may ponder the psychological significance of the denial of the natural father.

Whitland On that point, I should like to remind you of what seems a rather sweeping rejection of physical fatherhood in Matthew's Gospel. Jesus is talking to 'the crowds and his disciples', and he tells them, 'Do not call anyone on earth your father, because you have one Father, the one in the sky.'

Kamada I notice that you say 'the one in the sky', and not 'the one in heaven'.

Whitland Yes. It's my way — intended to be polite — of reminding you of the scheme of things, as Jesus' audience and the first readers of the Gospels would have envisaged them. And I'm trying to convey some of the flavour of the original Greek that the Gospels are written in.

Kamada My own academic background prompts me to explore the family relationships of Jesus in more detail. Mary, his mother, is a cult figure for many Christians, and it would interest me to see what the Gospels tell us about her. I know that Dr Hiraoka would like to be with us when we talk about that. I don't suppose she will intervene, but do not be misled by her apparent shyness. Behind her demure looks there is an ardent feminist.

Chapter 4

☞

Jesus and his mother

Kamada You have already met Dr Masako Hiraoka. Since her premature retirement from the readership in comparative cult studies at our University, she has kindly agreed to help me in my research.

Whitland [*Introduces himself in halting Japanese. He then adds in English*]: How are you?

Hiraoka Yes, I am well, thank you.

Kamada We have seen how Jesus — or the Gospel writers, at any rate — rejected his natural father, Joseph. But how do the Gospels describe his relationship with his mother, Mary? Dr Hiraoka is particularly interested in this question.

Whitland It is Luke who has the most to say about her, and one can also say that, among the four Gospel writers, Luke is generally the most favourably disposed towards women. But perhaps we should look at Mark first.

Kamada Yes, as Mark is the earliest of the four — historically speaking, the first Gospel — and as Matthew and Luke seem to have drawn on him when they came to write their own Gospels, let us begin with him.

Whitland Then, to my mind it's striking that in the first reference to Mary in the first Gospel to have been written, the author of that Gospel does not name her, and he represents Jesus as disowning her.

This is the incident where Jesus was preaching in a house, and his family set out to take charge of him, because they thought he was out of his mind. When they arrived at the house, they could not come in — it was too packed. So Jesus was told that his mother and brothers and sisters were outside, asking for him, and he replied, 'Who is my mother? Who are my brothers and sisters?' He then takes in with his glance the assembled company sitting in a circle round him and says, 'Look! My mother and my brothers! Because whoever does the will of God is my brother and sister and mother.'

Kamada We have seen why he could not include his father in that circle.

Whitland Well, no... But the question 'Who is my mother?' is also a dismissal, isn't it? *[Dr Hiraoka apparently indicates her agreement.]* And although we may not be able to capture the tone of voice, the wording is curt. And apart from this cold reference early on in Mark, Mary does not appear in person again in that Gospel — she is not even present at the execution of Jesus by the Romans, the crucifixion — but she is mentioned as the mother of Jesus on the occasion of a visit by Jesus to his native town.

I need not say much about Matthew in this regard. His account of the birth of Jesus is much simpler than Luke's, but like Luke, he reports that Mary was made pregnant by the Holy Spirit. So I will go straight on to Luke.

Luke's version of the birth of Jesus is the starting-point of most of the Christian tradition about Mary. It is here that the angel Gabriel — one of God's chief messengers — is sent by God to the town of Nazareth to tell Mary, 'a virgin engaged to a man, whose name was

Joseph, a descendant of David' that she will 'conceive in her womb, and give birth to a son, and call him Jesus'.

The angel goes on to tell Mary that her son will be great, and will be called:

> *The Son of the Most High; and the Lord God will give him the throne of his ancestor David; and he will be king over the House of Jacob for eternity, and there will be no end to his reign.*

Kamada [*Says something in Japanese to Dr Hiraoka.*] His ancestor, King David again!

Whitland To add to the confusion, the Greek word is simply 'father'.

Kamada And the House of Jacob?

Whitland It simply means Israel. But let me remind you of Mary's reply to the angel: 'How will this happen, since I do not know a man?'

Mary means that she has not slept with a man — this is what the word 'know' meant in Hebrew in such a context: in the Old Testament it is recorded that Adam 'knew Eve, his wife, and she conceived and gave birth to Cain'.

The angel answered Mary and said: 'The Holy Spirit will come upon you, and the power of the Most High will cast its shadow on you, and this is why the child will be holy and will be called Son of God.'

Mary told the angel: 'Look, I am the Lord's servant. Let it happen to me according to what you have said.' And the angel left her.

Mary now goes to visit her cousin Elizabeth, who greets Mary as 'the mother of my Lord', and this prompts the hymn which most manuscripts of the Gospels ascribe to Mary (although some, to Elizabeth), known in the Christian tradition as the Magnificat, from the Latin translation of its opening words, 'My soul proclaims the greatness of the Lord.'

Kamada Yes, the Magnificat. It is a song, isn't it?

Hiraoka There is music by Bach.

Whitland Yes, Bach really is magnificent! But Luke continues the story with the actual birth of Jesus, Mary's 'first-born son'. Here is Mary wrapping the baby in long strips of cloth and putting him in an animal's feeding-trough, because there was no other place to put him (though the two oxen you may have seen on Christmas cards do not appear in Luke, but are a later legendary addition). But the shepherds watching their flocks by night are also in Luke, and it is their story that Mary 'keeps and ponders in her heart'.

In accordance with ancient Jewish law, forty days after the birth of Jesus, Mary's blood had to be purified, and Mary and Joseph took the baby to Jerusalem to present him, as 'the male child opening the womb' to the Lord. A just and devout man called Simeon who was living in Jerusalem came to the Temple, at the prompting of the Holy Spirit, and took Jesus in his arms, and hailed him as God's salvation, prepared by God in the face of every people, 'a light of revelation for non-Jews, and the glory of God's people, Israel.'

Then, as the child's father and mother were amazed at these remarks, Simeon blessed them...

Kamada Excuse me. Did you say they were amazed? That is strange to me, after all that Mary had been told by the angel, and by her cousin Elizabeth. Not to mention the shepherds. Why were they amazed?

Whitland Luke simply says they were amazed. It is a word he is fond of, and perhaps he just wants to say that they were impressed.

But in any event, Simeon told Mary: 'Look, this child is destined for the fall and rise of many in Israel, and to be a sign that is disputed; and a sword will go through your soul, as well.'

Hiraoka A sword will go through your soul? What does that mean?

Whitland It is a reference to Mary's witness of Jesus' agonising death by crucifixion. These words have also inspired several composers, especially Italian, to set to music a medieval hymn commemorating the sorrow of Mary at that time. But strangely enough, Luke does not say, when he describes the crucifixion, that Mary was present, and he seems to imply, in his account of Jesus' resurrection, that she was not there.

In fact, after the birth narrative, Mary all but disappears from Luke's Gospel. There is only a mention or two, apart from the incident of the twelve-year-old Jesus in the Temple where, in spite of all that happened at Jesus' conception and birth, Mary is puzzled by her son's remark about his Father's concerns, and indeed, in admonishing Jesus, refers to Joseph — perhaps only out of deference — as 'your father'.

There is one further indirect reference to Mary, however, in Luke, which ought to be mentioned. I am going to translate it literally, because I find that modern English translations are not so earthy as the original Greek, even though the seventeenth-century *King James Version* does it full justice.

When a woman in the crowd listening to Jesus preach cries out: 'Blessed is the womb that carried you, and the breasts that you sucked!' Jesus replies in very much the same words as in the incident in the packed house: 'Blessed are they who hear the word of God and keep it!'

Kamada It is remarkable, isn't it, that once again, Jesus denies here the importance and the validity of the natural tie, the flesh and blood tie.

Whitland Yes, but as we shall have other occasions to talk about that, if you agree, we'll look finally at John's account of Mary, which is particularly notable for being the only Gospel to report Mary's presence at the crucifixion of Jesus.

In John's Gospel, the one believed by a majority of scholars to have been composed a couple of generations after the events it describes, Mary appears twice. The first occasion is at Cana, the village where Jesus performed the 'first of the signs that revealed his glory'.

There was a wedding at Cana in Galilee, and Jesus' mother was there. By the way, John does not name her. Jesus and his disciples were also invited. According to John, the supply of wine gave out...

Hiraoka *Sumimasen!* Gave out?

Whitland The wine had all been drunk.

Kamada It was a good wedding!

Whitland Certainly! And, writes John,

> *when there was no more wine, Jesus' mother says to him, 'They have no wine.' And Jesus says to her, 'What has that got to do with me and you, woman? My time hasn't come yet.' His mother says to the servants, 'Do whatever he tells you.'*

You see, I am keeping the tenses of the original Greek. I don't know how that will strike you, but this is also the style of folk stories of the kind you can still hear in Greek villages. These stories, too, tend to take quite miraculous events in their stride, and when John goes on to describe how Jesus then turns about 120 gallons of water into the best wine served at the wedding, he does so in quite a matter-of-fact way.

Kamada A moment, please! Dr Hiraoka and I would like to know if you are saying that this story in John's Gospel is some kind of folk tale.

Whitland It is more than that. You can see, after all, that the miracle it describes has a symbolic meaning that has been well remarked by commentators. For one thing, although Jesus is only a guest, it is suggested elsewhere in the Gospels that Jesus himself is the divine bridegroom, and in later Christian belief his Church is said to be his bride.

But as we are particularly concerned at the moment with Jesus' relationship with his mother, as shown in the Gospels, what interests us immediately here is the way Jesus talks to his mother, addressing her curtly as 'woman' — *gunai*, in Greek. This is the word, incidentally, at the root of the English words 'misogynist' and 'gynaecology'.

According to some scholars, this is an unusual way for a son to talk to his mother, although it is the word used on the only other occasion in the Gospels that Jesus addresses his mother. And however unusual it may be, I have found an interesting parallel in the Greek tragedian Sophocles' masterpiece, *King Oedipus*, which had its first performance about 500 years before the miracle at Cana. When Oedipus first realises the truth of his situation, that he has slept with his own mother, Queen Jocasta, he addresses her, too, as *gunai*. It is certainly not a warm or affectionate word, but it may imply a certain respect.

In John's Gospel, Jesus addresses a Samaritan woman that he meets by chance at a well as 'woman', and also the woman caught committing adultery — one of these days we shall have to talk about that incident — and one sometimes gets the impression that the word, used in this way, comes near to the English word 'madam', which can also trail a certain ambiguity, and depends for its exact meaning on the tone of voice as much as the context.

Hiraoka Can I understand from what you say that in both these cases — I mean the meeting with the woman at the well, and the woman caught in adultery — these women were strangers to Jesus? If this is so, it is striking that Jesus addresses his own mother in the same way.

Whitland Yes, it is! And it is not only the word 'woman' that is curt, but the whole sentence, which runs in the Greek: 'What is it to me and to you, woman?' Again, however, we miss the tone of voice. There may even be a kind of light-hearted humour in it: to this day you can hear jokey anecdotes, some of them part of local folklore, in the eastern Mediterranean — I mean in Greece and Turkey — that play on this 'what's it to me or you?' theme.

Kamada [*With an apology to Whitland, says something in Japanese to Dr Hiraoka.*]

Whitland There could hardly be a more stark contrast between the scene at Cana and the only other occasion on which Mary appears in John's Gospel. This is the crucifixion. And this is how John narrates Mary's part in the drama:

> *Near the cross of Jesus stood his mother and his mother's sister, Mary the wife of Clopas, and Mary of Magdala. So Jesus, seeing his mother, and the disciple that he loved standing nearby, says to his mother, 'Woman, look, your son!' Then he says to the disciple, 'Look, your mother!' And from that hour the disciple took her into his own home.*

John is the only Gospel writer to say that Mary, the mother of Jesus, was present at the crucifixion. But again, he does not name her, although he does name two other women, both also called Mary, who were there with her. Indeed, John's account of the women at the crucifixion is remarkable for its brevity. There is no attempt to describe their feelings.

Again, Jesus is reported to have addressed his mother as 'woman', which on the face of it seems bleak, even when uttered by a man dying in agony. But the editors of *The New Jerusalem Bible* claim that what they call 'the unusual term "woman"' amounts to 'a declaration that

Mary, the new Eve, is the spiritual mother of all the faithful.'

That may seem rather a lot to read into one simple word, but these same editors, noting that Jesus addresses his mother as 'woman' in both the passages in John's Gospel where she appears, express the opinion that John repeated this detail on purpose, and implied a link with the verse in the Old Testament where 'the woman' Eve is said to be the mother of all living people.

Kamada When the editors you have just quoted talk of Mary as 'the spiritual mother of all the faithful', they are speaking of the cultic Mary of later Christianity, aren't they? But if you have given a true account of Jesus' relation to his mother, as portrayed in the Gospels, there hardly seems to be any preparation there for this cult.

Whitland Perhaps not, but at the same time, it is not strictly true, as one modern writer has asserted, that in the New Testament, 'Mary was in no way elevated beyond the sphere of ordinary human beings.' But apart from the role Mary plays in the largely mythical stories of Jesus' birth — the Nativity with a capital N, as it is known in most of Christendom — in Matthew and Luke, she makes only rare and brief appearances in the Gospels.

The other Gospels, Mark and John, have no nativity story, and take little account of Mary. As Marina Warner remarks in her scholarly book on the cult of the Virgin Mary, 'In Mark... she appears once in an unflattering light, and is mentioned only once as the mother of Jesus.' And, as we have seen, Mary also appears only twice in John's Gospel, once at the wedding feast where Jesus turned the water into wine, and once at the crucifixion.

Kamada I think that this cult is a problem for some Christians.

Whitland Or one could say that some Christian sects do not entertain this cult. But Luke states quite clearly that Mary was a virgin — *parthenos* in Greek — when Jesus was born, and in Orthodox and Roman Catholic belief, she is a perpetual virgin. This doctrine, however, was not given the Church's official stamp until 553 AD, when the fifth Ecumenical Council, meeting in Constantinople, declared that Mary was 'a virgin for ever'.

Objections have been raised to the doctrine that Mary was — or is — a perpetual virgin, because a verse in Matthew's Gospel says that Joseph had no intercourse with Mary until she had given birth to a son, which implies rather clearly that he did have intercourse with her after this event. Even if some commentators have not accepted this implication, there is the awkward fact that some manuscripts even write of Mary's first-born son in this context, which again implies on the face of it that she had other sons after Jesus.

Then there are the references to Jesus' brothers and sisters in the Gospels. Those who still maintain Mary's perpetual virginity say that the words 'brothers' and 'sisters' used in these Gospel passages can also mean 'half-brother', 'cousin' or 'near relative'.

The head of the Roman Catholic Church, Pope John Paul II, has declared that Jesus was Mary's only child, and that she was a virgin both before and after his birth. And according to the Pope, there was no word for 'cousin' in either Hebrew or Aramaic, and the expression 'first-born son' was a term in Jewish law that meant a woman's first child, regardless of whether she had others later.

Kamada It is apparent that the Pope has examined this question in great depth.

Whitland Mary's perpetual virginity is not the only feature of her cult, however. In fact, 'Perpetual Virgin' was not even the first title conferred on Mary during the centuries, after the Gospels were written, in which Christian dogma was being formulated.

When the first general council of the Church met at Nicaea — the present-day Iznik, in north-west Turkey — in the year 325 of our era, it adopted the dogma that Jesus, the son of God, was born of the Father before time began. This is a notion already hinted at in John's Gospel, where Jesus claims that he existed before Abraham, the founder of the Hebrew people. And this Nicaean doctrine led in turn to the attribution to Mary of the title *Theotokos* — a Greek word meaning 'God-bearer' or 'Mother of God'.

Kamada This is also a very difficult notion.

Whitland Well even at the time, various people objected to this title, including the fourth-century Roman Emperor Julian and, later, Nestorius, the bishop of Constantinople, who remarked that he could not think of God as two or three weeks old, and was condemned to exile by the Council of Ephesus for his trouble in the year 431.

But by this time, many Christians were already praying to Mary, and representations of her in pictures began to play a great and ever more prominent role. As a writer I have already quoted once today expresses it, 'From a recipient of grace, Mary became the dispenser of grace with a benignity not even attributed to Christ himself.'

This may seem an exaggerated claim, but in the Greek Orthodox Church, to this day, Mary is called 'Mother of God', 'Eternal Virgin', and 'All-Holy', although the last title — the most commonly heard in Greece nowadays — is not dogmatically defined. And although many Orthodox and Roman Catholic believers devote more time to paying their respects to Mary than in praying to God, in both churches a distinction is made between *venerating* the Virgin Mary and *worshipping* God.

In other words, Mary may be the Mother of God, but she is not divine — she is still human. But in both churches, prayers are addressed to Mary, in the belief that she will intercede with God on behalf of mortal sinners.

Kamada Mary is a powerful figure for these Christians — surely above... how did you express it?

Whitland Above the sphere of ordinary human beings? Yes, whatever the Gospel view of her. And I could add that many scholarly articles and books have been published, aiming to show that in her historical progress, Mary absorbed the attributes and claimed the worship of various pagan goddesses displaced by Christianity.

Chapter 5

Jesus' brothers and sisters

Kamada You referred a little while ago to Jesus' brothers and sisters. Dr Hiraoka would like to know more about them, especially his sisters.

Whitland Yes, they are mentioned more than once in the Gospels. I've already referred to the occasion when they arrive with Jesus' mother at a house where he is teaching. That's described in Mark's Gospel, where they are not named. But in another passage in Mark, the brothers are actually named.

On this occasion, Jesus has been teaching in a synagogue, and his audience, astonished at his wisdom and at the miracles he has performed, ask, 'Isn't he the carpenter, the son of Mary and brother of Jacob and Joset and Judas and Simon? And aren't his sisters here with us?'

Hiraoka *Dozo...* And the sisters. What were their names?

Whitland His sisters are not named. In a way, this highlights a curious area of discrimination between men and women in the world of the Gospels: there is an abundance of names for men, but a great shortage of names for women.

Kamada Yes, Dr Hiraoka has been investigating this phenomenon.

Hiraoka I was perplexed by the number of Marys in the Gospels. There seem to be five different women called Mary.

Whitland Yes, and the Gospel writers themselves don't seem to have sorted them out completely.

Kamada According to Dr Hiraoka's count, there are in the Gospels about fifteen times as many men's names as women's.

Hiraoka If we include the ancestral names in Matthew and Luke's genealogies of Jesus with other men's names reported in the Gospels, we arrive at a total of about 120 different names for men. But only eight women's names occur. And even disregarding the great ancestral lists, it can be said that nearly six times as many men as women are named.

Kamada Dr Hiraoka is interested in statistics.

Whitland I like them, too — in moderation, of course. Figures sometimes speak louder than words. The writers of the Gospels were not interested in them at all in that sense. For them, the only figures that mattered were symbolic: three, seven, twelve, forty and seventy. Even when they give what looks like an accurate figure, it usually turns out to be symbolic, like the miraculous catch of 153 fishes at the end of John's Gospel, although in this case we can't be sure what is being symbolised.

But what I find more interesting than these general figures about women's names is that some individual women, like Jesus' sisters, who could be important, display such a remarkable ability to remain anonymous.

A very striking example is presented by the woman in Bethany who poured expensive perfume over Jesus. In spite, in her case, of being promised future fame, there is not so much as a passing mention of her name.

Another woman who remains mysteriously anonymous is referred to as 'the mother of Zebedee's sons' — but she is, as far as I can see, the only woman in the Gospels to be identified in such a way, although I have been told that this was quite a usual way of referring to a woman in Gospel times.

Chapter 6

☙

Jesus against the blood family

Whitland According to the Gospels, Jesus disowned his earthly father, was cool towards his mother, and would not recognise his brothers and sisters. It would be an understatement to say that he was not a family man in the accepted sense.

Kamada Accepted by whom? The notions of what constitutes a family vary a lot, don't they, from one society to another?

Whitland Yes, they do. And I'm ready to admit that in some societies or cultures, as anthropologists call them, there may not even be a word for 'family' in the sense that an Italian, say, might use the word *famiglia*.

Kamada Even our Japanese word, *kazoku*, often conveys more of the sense of the English words 'house' or 'household'.

Whitland That's interesting, because the same is true of the Greek words *oikos* and *oikia* in the Gospels. And on that basis, I could say that Jesus has no word in his vocabulary that corresponds closely to the English word 'family'. But in every society, let's say, there is an idea of a more or less closely-knit group held together by ties of blood or adoption that is the important, basic social unit. Would you agree with that?

Kamada Certainly. And it is this kind of social unit that the Jesus of the Gospels seems to be rejecting. Is that what you are saying?

Whitland Yes. If we look at Jesus as a man, there is nothing in the Gospels to suggest that he ever married or fathered children, even though some modern writers say this does not prove that he did not marry. In any case, his style of life as a wandering preacher, with 'nowhere', as he himself said, 'to rest his head' hardly lent itself to ordinary domesticity, and his words as well as his deeds express a rejection of regular family life, not only for himself, but for his followers.

In the story in Mark's Gospel that we've already talked about, Jesus declares that his real brothers, sisters and mother are those who do God's will. This has led some Christians to speak of Jesus' spiritual family, as distinct from a physical or blood family.

There can be no objection to that, so long as when the word 'family' is used without qualification, it is made clear which kind of family, the spiritual or the physical, is meant. But nowadays, when churchmen and politicians in Christendom talk, as they often do, about the family and Christian values, they are seldom if ever referring to the spiritual family.

On the contrary, they are usually claiming that the Christian church is committed to maintaining and cherishing the family in its usual modern western sense of parents and their offspring, forming a tight-knit group for mutual support and, incidentally, leading a law-abiding and socially responsible life.

But whatever the various churches' commitment to the family as a tangible and stable institution, there is no such commitment in the Gospels. On the contrary, the Gospels abound in open hostility to the blood family as an institution. The most extreme passage, and one which has given translators and commentators the most obvious problems, is to be found in Luke:

If anyone comes to me, and does not hate his father, and his mother, and his wife, and his children, and his brothers and his sisters, and even his own soul, he cannot be my disciple.

Kamada Hate! *Kirau?* Please excuse me. *(He and Dr Hiraoka exchange some words in Japanese.)* Did you say 'hate'?

Whitland I am sorry, but I must insist that the word used here certainly is 'hate'. In Greek it is *misei*, a word that is one root of the English word 'misanthropist' — someone with no love for the human race.

Hiraoka Or 'misogynist' — a man who hates women, isn't that so?

Whitland Yes, indeed! I'm impressed by your reaction to the word 'hate' on Jesus' lips. Because it has often created difficulties for Bible readers, but especially for translators and commentators.

One modern translator tries to soften the word by putting it in inverted commas: 'If anyone comes to me without "hating" his father and mother...' But there is no justification for this in the Greek text, and in any case, much as English expounders of the New Testament love them, inverted commas had not been invented when the Gospels were written.

Another modern translation keeps the word 'hating', but in a footnote says some special feature of the Hebrew language is behind the word: 'Jesus asks, not for hate,' this translator claims, 'but for total detachment now.'

Apart from the obvious difficulty that hatred is one thing, and total detachment a completely different thing, I have a particular problem with this learned translator's commentary. Because Luke was not writing for an audience with a knowledge of Hebrew. He was writing, as another modern scholar puts it, 'with an eye on intelligent Gentile (non-Jewish, that is to say) readers'. So these readers would surely have taken the Greek words in their normal sense.

But it's not only modern readers who have a problem with this passage in Luke. Matthew presents this saying of Jesus in a noticeably watered-down form:

He who has more love for his father or mother than for me is not
worthy of me. And he who loves his son or daughter more than me
is not worthy of me.

This notion is presented elsewhere in Matthew's Gospel in another form, when Jesus tells his disciples:

Everyone who has left houses, or brothers, or sisters, or father, or
mother, or wife, or children, or land for my sake will receive a hundred
times as much and will inherit eternal life.

Yet another occasion on which Jesus repudiated the ordinary Jewish sense of family obligations was when he told a man to follow him, but the man said he wanted to go and bury his father first. Jesus replied: 'Let the dead bury the dead.' Another man asked if he could say goodbye to the folks at home first and he, too, got a dusty answer from Jesus.

Kamada This is also striking. I mean, that Jesus' remarks run so counter to traditional Jewish ideas.

Whitland Yes, but I should also mention that some scholars do question whether Jesus actually did express such downright hostility to the blood family. They believe that these sayings reflect the struggle, after Jesus' death, of the early Christians to break away from mainstream Judaism.

As one modern commentator puts it: 'The Gospels come from a time when rivalry between church and synagogue was very acute.' In the course of this struggle, many families must have split up. So, if the Gospel writers are projecting the concerns of their own time onto Jesus, and putting words into his mouth, what these extreme sayings really mean is: 'It's more important to come over to us than to stick to your family.'

Kamada The twentieth century has witnessed a number of regimes that have adopted the same sort of slogan.

Whitland Yes, and this theme, of the break-up of families, is given, in some other passages in the Gospels, a sinister twist that reminds us of what has happened under some totalitarian regimes in our own time.

In Mark, in the highly coloured passage in which Jesus predicts the end of this world and the arrival of the Son of Man — I suppose he really means the Son of God — on the clouds, he tells the disciples:

> *Brother will betray brother to death, and father will betray child.*
> *And children will revolt against their parents, and put them to death.*

But Luke, in spite of having some of the most extreme anti-family sayings elsewhere, apparently did not care much for this idea of children killing their parents, because he leaves it out in his report of this prophecy.

But if Luke draws the line at children murdering their parents, he does report another of Jesus' outbursts, where he says he has come to set the earth on fire, and goes on:

> *Do you think I came to give peace on earth? No, I tell you, but rather*
> *to bring dissension. From now on there will be five in one house*
> *divided three against two and two against three. They will be divided*
> *father against son, and son against father; mother against daughter,*
> *and daughter against mother; mother-in-law against her daughter-in-*
> *law, and daughter-in-law against mother-in-law.*

Hiraoka Daughter-in-law against mother-in-law? That's interesting!

Whitland Especially as it does not look as if mothers-in-law loomed particularly large in Jesus' imagination. But in these remarks some readers of the Bible have found an echo of Micah, one of the Old Testament prophets, who lived in the eighth century BC So the question is, was Jesus consciously quoting Micah, or is Luke putting Micah's words into Jesus' mouth, as Mark may have done in this instance, but from a different source and a different motive? — I mean, as part of his purpose, in writing the Gospel, to portray Jesus as a faithful upholder of the Jewish religion, as a prophet continuing the Hebrew tradition.

Chapter 7

Jesus rules out divorce

Kamada The last time we met, the day before yesterday, I think you said that the Christian churches insist on the value of the physical family, in spite of what Jesus had to say on the subject.

Whitland Yes, I'm sure I said something to that effect.

Kamada But Dr Hiraoka has pointed out to me that in the Gospels, Jesus does insist that the marriage tie is sacred, and he rules divorce right out. That makes a problem for me. I find these two doctrines contradictory.

Whitland Masako — Dr Hiraoka, I mean, is right. I think Jesus, the Jesus of the Gospels, is adamant against divorce. His attitude towards it is shown at its most uncompromising in Mark's Gospel, where some Jews who regarded themselves as interpreters both of the sacred writings and the traditions handed down by word of mouth come to test Jesus with the question, 'Is a man allowed to divorce his wife?' Then these same men who ask this question say that Moses, the legendary Israelite leader and first great lawgiver, did allow a man to write a bill of divorce.

Jesus replies that this was merely Moses' concession to 'your hard-heartedness', and he goes on, 'but from the beginning of creation, God made them male and female. For this reason, a man shall leave his father and mother, and stick to his wife, and the two shall become one flesh. So they are no longer two, but one flesh. So what God has joined together, no man may separate.'

Hiraoka *Sumimasen*! These words are in the Christian marriage ritual, aren't they?

Whitland Yes, you are right. And the emphasis on 'one flesh' is momentous. So, later in the same chapter of Mark, Jesus links divorce directly with adultery:

> *Whoever divorces his wife and marries another, commits adultery against her; and if she, after divorcing her husband, marries someone else, she commits adultery.*

In two almost identical passages, Matthew also makes Jesus link divorce directly with adultery, but according to him, Jesus allowed an exception:

> *every man who divorces his wife, except for reasons of* porneia, *makes her commit adultery.*

Kamada [*Says something in Japanese and Dr Hiraoka answers him.*] Except for reasons...

Whitland I'm sorry, I quoted the Greek word *porneia*, which originally means 'prostitution', and is connected, of course, with the English word 'pornography'.

Kamada [*He laughs, but it could be from embarrassment, rather than amusement.*] And the Japanese word *poruno*.

Whitland That must be an American import! But as for the word in Matthew, the Christian churches apparently disagree about its meaning. The Greek Orthodox and the Protestant churches take it to mean fornication within the marriage, which would mean that the woman had already committed adultery, and that in these circumstances, divorce is permitted. To some leading Roman Catholic scholars, however, *porneia* in this context seems more likely to refer to incest — the possibilities of committing it are spelt out at length in the Old Testament.

In general, in the Gospels, Jesus expresses a particular horror of adultery. In one passage in Matthew, he mentions adultery in the same breath as murder; and his prohibition of divorce appeals to no other argument than that it leads to adultery.

In the Old Testament, too, in both versions of the Ten Commandments, the fundamental ethical rules of the ancient Jews, adultery is also mentioned immediately after murder (and immediately before theft) as a forbidden activity. Biblical scholars seem to agree that adultery in the ancient Jewish view did not refer to any sort of sexual act outside marriage, but only to a married man sleeping with another man's wife, or to the woman in this situation.

Kamada And in the Jewish view — the Christian view, too — these distinctions — the ones you have just mentioned — are as important to the God who created everything as the distinction Jesus says he made from the beginning of creation between male and female?

Whitland I am far from being qualified to answer you. You must ask an expert on God — a theologian, I mean. But Jesus himself apparently widened the definition of adultery, rather than refining it or narrowing it down. I am thinking of one of the most famous of his sayings, in the sermon he preached on a mountain, that is reported by Matthew. There Jesus goes beyond any traditional definition of adultery to include feelings or thoughts as well as acts, and any libidinous thoughts that a man might have towards any woman, whether married or not:

> *You have heard that it has been said, 'You shall not commit adultery.'*
> *But I say to you, that every man who looks at a woman with desire*
> *has already committed adultery with her in her heart.*

Hiraoka On the other hand, he is indulgent towards the woman caught in the very act of adultery.

Whitland He certainly saves her from being stoned to death — a luminous example of not condemning the sinner, even though on other occasions he has condemned the sin.

Hiraoka So how do Jesus' views on adultery and divorce square with his general attitude towards the physical family?

Whitland The obvious answer seems to be that they do not. Biblical commentators have also drawn attention to Jesus' insistence on the sacredness of the commandment to honour your father and your mother, which again is not easily reconciled with his general hostility to the physical family, the blood family, and the curt answer, in particular, that he gave to the man who wanted to bury his father before coming to follow him.

Up to now, I have not seen any discussion of the apparent conflict between these different sayings of Jesus, so I shall be grateful if, in your research, either of you find any relevant commentary.

One point that does seem significant to me is that the sayings which appear to support the structure of the physical family are all either quotations from the Old Testament or set in the context of such quotations, whereas the anti-family sayings are almost all original with Jesus.

Hiraoka But if I have understood everything you have said, the absolute ruling out of divorce is also particular to Jesus.

Whitland Yes, that is difficult. But I think there is also, underlying all the sayings about the family, a distinction between the present world and its obligations, and the world that Jesus calls the Kingdom of Heaven. According to Jesus, in this Kingdom there is no place for the blood family and the sexual acts that bring it into existence and subsequently either maintain it or threaten it.

Chapter 8

☞

Jesus rescues a woman
from stoning

Whitland You mentioned last time, Dr Hiraoka, Jesus' indulgence towards the woman caught in the act of adultery. This is a remarkable episode on several counts, but perhaps I should begin by mentioning that, as a self-contained story, so to speak, it has no fixed place in the ancient manuscripts of the New Testament. I believe, however, that most modern scholars take it to be an authentic element of the Gospels, even if there are varying views as to its authorship.

Kamada My understanding is that the Gospels do not always assign specific contexts to the deeds and sayings that they relate so indications of time, except in the very last days of Jesus' life, are indefinite.

Whitland It was an age before timetables. There was hardly any way that dates and times could be a feature of the traditions about Jesus. However that may be, this famous incident that we are talking about is to be found only in some Greek manuscripts of John's Gospel, but on stylistic grounds his authorship has been ruled out. Some scholars think the author may have been Luke, while others are inclined to attribute it to a later editor of John.

Kamada In any case, perhaps you could tell us what those Greek manuscripts say.

Whitland Yes, it is not a long story, and this is how it reads:

> *And Jesus went to the Mount of Olives. And at dawn he was again present at the Temple, and all the people began to come to him; and he sat down and taught them.*
>
> *And the scribes and Pharisees bring a woman who had been caught committing adultery. They stood her in the middle, and say to him, 'Teacher, this woman has been caught in the act of adultery. And in the Law, Moses orders us to stone such women to death. So what do you say about her?' They asked him to put him to the test, so that they would be able to accuse him. But Jesus bent down and began to write on the ground with his finger.*
>
> *And as they insisted on their question, he looked up, and said to them: 'Let the one among you who is without sin be the first to throw a stone at her.' Then he bent down again and went on writing on the ground.*
>
> *When they heard his answer, they began to go away one by one, starting with the older ones, until the last, and Jesus was left alone with the woman in the middle. And Jesus straightened up and said to her, 'Woman, where are they? Did no one condemn you?' And she said, 'No one, Sir.' And Jesus said, 'Neither do I condemn you. Go, and do not sin from now on.'*

Hiraoka It is a most beautiful story.

Whitland Yes! And although the manuscript authority for this incident is so questionable, it does have an authentic ring. Jesus' reported behaviour of writing in the dust with his finger and giving such a memorable, aphoristic challenge to the woman's accusers are actions of an originality beyond the scope of any secondary compiler or editor to invent.

The Pharisees are shown in the story as trying to set a trap for

Jesus. As John Marsh explains in his massive commentary *The Gospel of Saint John*, if Jesus recommended stoning, the Pharisees could report him to the Roman authorities as a man inciting to murder or riot; if he advised them to let the woman go, he could be denounced as a Rabbi who did not care for the sacred law of Moses.

The ancient Jewish law prescribing penalties for adultery is set out in detail in the Old Testament book *Deuteronomy*, in an interesting chapter which lumps together, without any specific discrimination, rules against cross-dressing and wanton bird-nesting, a prohibition against clothing made partly of wool and partly of linen, and the imposition of the death penalty on adulterers.

But death by stoning is laid down only for a virgin, engaged to one man, but having sexual intercourse with another; and even in this case it is specified that the illicit act must have taken place in a town, where the girl could have called for help. Only the man must die in the case of a rape in open country. If a young virgin who is not engaged is raped, the rapist must make a substantial payment in silver to her father, marry her, and never divorce her.

Kamada The taboos you referred to are interesting... Bird-nesting and cross-dressing! But to the primitive, prelogical mind that conceived them, there was a logical connexion of some kind between them. They all relate to activities where things of one sort or another are mixed.

But more to our present purpose, I believe Dr Hiraoka would like to know something about the partner of the woman that Jesus saved from stoning. Where was he? And where are the witnesses to the act?

Whitland That we are not told. And you could say the story does betray a masculine bias, although not an unusual one for that time. But, in spite of those ancient prejudices, I hope you agree with Dr Hiraoka that there is great beauty in the story.

Chapter 9

☞

Jesus and the Kingdom of God

Kamada At one of our meetings, you spoke of a divide between this world — the world we live in — and the world that Jesus called the Kingdom of Heaven. This, as I understand from what I have read, is the same as the Kingdom of God. It is one of the basic themes, one of the most persistent themes, of Jesus' teaching, but I have not been able to form a very clear idea of it.

Whitland Yes, the Kingdom of Heaven and the Kingdom of God are the same. Matthew almost always uses the expression 'the Kingdom of the Heavens' (or 'the Kingdom of the Skies'), while the other Gospel writers call it 'the Kingdom of God'. Perhaps the two forms both derive from a passage in the Old Testament prophet Daniel, who predicts that the God of heaven will set up a kingdom which will not be destroyed for eternity. Daniel does not say much about this kingdom — in fact, he says hardly anything about it, but he seems to envisage it as some kind of superpower, which every other authority will kowtow to.

Kamada So is it one kingdom among many?

Whitland Apparently. But one could say that it gets only a couple of passing references in Daniel, and Jesus seems to have been the first Jewish teacher to bring the Kingdom of God into the centre of his teaching. But — how can I put it? His ideas on the subject, as reported by the Gospel writers, who perhaps couldn't completely grasp them — his ideas are not all of a piece.

In his remarkable book *The Historical Figure of Jesus*, the American scholar Professor E. P. Sanders divides Jesus' sayings about the Kingdom into six categories. I hope I'm not oversimplifying the whole subject too outrageously if I say that Jesus usually, but not always, speaks of the Kingdom as something in the future, and he usually, though not always, speaks of it as something transcendent — as something, in other words, that is not of this world.

So this has led to a sharp divide among Christians: some think the Kingdom of God can be realised on this planet, and it follows from this that they interpret Jesus' teaching as a blueprint for social reform. Others say this is nonsense, and they believe that any attempt to bring about the Kingdom here on earth is doomed not so much to simple failure as to the promotion of a totalitarian monstrosity.

Kamada We certainly have two diametrically opposed views here. And you are saying that both these views can, in fact, be derived from what Jesus says?

Whitland Yes. As I say, this is spelt out in detail in Professor Sanders' book. I think it's likely that the individual listener's or reader's response to the various sayings in the Gospels on this subject will depend on that individual's temperament, interests, and psychological needs. But on the whole, I have the impression that those who have studied the question most deeply incline to the view that Jesus preaches the Kingdom as transcendent — as otherworldly. In John's Gospel, Jesus tells the Roman governor of Judaea quite unambiguously that his royal status is not from this world.

It's true that Jesus talks about eating and drinking and sitting on thrones in the Kingdom of God, but he never elaborates on the delights to be enjoyed there. Rudolf Bultmann warns his readers that words like 'realm' or 'kingdom' can carry connotations for a modern reader of citizens and members of the state, or of fellow-countrymen, that are misleading when applied to Jesus' conception of the Kingdom of God. 'The Kingdom of God', writes Bultmann, 'is not an ideal which realises itself in human history; we cannot speak of its founding, its building, its completion; we can only say that it draws near, it comes, it appears.'

Kamada Does this mean that this present world cannot be the scene of an ideal or perfect state, whatever you want to call that state — enlightenment or salvation?

Whitland Yes, according to Bultmann, and others who think like him. His interpretation implies to my mind an essentially pessimistic view of this world, and one that is not altogether incompatible with the dualistic belief to be found in some later Christian heresies that the present world is a kingdom of darkness, and the world to come, a kingdom of light. Isn't there a glimpse of this dualism when Jesus explains to his disciples his own parable of the weeds that grow in wheat fields?

Kamada I do not recall this parable.

Whitland It is in Matthew's Gospel. Jesus compares the Kingdom of the Heavens to a farmer who sows some good seed in his field, and while he is asleep, his enemy comes and sows weeds among the wheat. Explaining the parable, Jesus says that the sower of the good seed is the deliverer awaited by the Jews; the field is the world; the good seed represents the children of the Kingdom; the weeds are the children of the Evil One; the enemy who sowed the weeds is the Devil; and the harvest is the end of the world. In John's Gospel, too, Jesus refers to Satan as 'the prince of this world'.

Kamada From what you say, and from my own reading of the Gospels, I am driven to the conclusion that whatever the Kingdom of God is or is not, it will — or perhaps does — displace or replace the present scheme of things. In other words, Jesus regards the present scheme of things as entirely dispensable. This seems to me an important point, and a fundamental one.

Whitland I am certainly not going to quarrel with that!

Chapter 10

☙

Jesus and the end of the world

Kamada Since our last meeting, I have looked at the parable of the weeds that you quoted then, and there is a question that I should like to ask. Jesus explains the harvest as 'the end of the age', or 'the end of the world' or even, in one translation, 'the end of time'. What does this mean?

Whitland We're into very deep water here — an ocean, in fact, which biblical scholars call eschatology. It's not a word in Jesus' vocabulary, but one used by theologians, especially German theologians in the last two centuries. It means discussion or thought about last things, about the end of the world, in other words. The learned Germans' interest in the subject is prompted by the fact that the Jews of Jesus' time expected God to intervene in their nation's history, as they believed he had done more than once in the past, but this time finally and decisively, in order to set up an earthly kingdom in which the land would be divided between the twelve original tribes of Israel.

Kamada You say, 'the Jews of Jesus' time'...

Whitland Well, I meant to include Jesus among them. He evidently shared this belief. In fact, he thought these events would come about very soon — in the lifetime of some of his disciples.
  According to Mark — and Matthew and Luke echo his words —

Jesus warned his disciples against false leaders or prophets, and predicted a period of 'wars and rumours of wars... nation against nation... earthquakes in some places... famines.' He then told them that they would be handed over to local courts and get a thrashing in synagogues.

Jesus goes on to quote from the Old Testament prophet Daniel, and says that when the disciples see a sick-making idol standing where it ought not to stand — he means, on holy ground — then those in the southern province of Israel, Judaea, should flee to the mountains.

'If a man is on the roof of his house, he should stay there,' says Jesus. You must picture a flat roof, of course. He then predicts particular suffering for pregnant or nursing women.

Hiraoka Excuse me, please. *[Says something in Japanese to Kamada.]*

Kamada Dr Hiraoka wonders why pregnant and nursing women should be singled out.

Whitland Perhaps simply because they actually would have an extra tough time in the conditions he is describing. But in some of the more lurid ancient Jewish prophecies, the prophet dwells on monstrous and untimely births, which are taken to be signs of impending calamities, and perhaps Jesus is influenced by these ideas.

Kamada Well, this speech by Jesus is also lurid, isn't it?

Whitland It's a strange mixture, certainly. I find it naïve that after this mention of pregnant women, Jesus advises his disciples to pray that all this does not happen in winter. Especially as he goes on to say that the sun will be darkened, which would make it rather wintry, in any case. What can one make of it?

He also says that the stars will come falling out of the sky, but a

modern author says we mustn't think that to Jesus' audience this
meant the end of the world. To their minds, he says, the stars were
quite small, as they are to young children, and could drop down to
earth without causing very serious trouble.

But Jesus ends his prophecy with a promise. After these dire events,
the promised liberator will arrive with great power and glory. He will
send God's messengers to gather his chosen people from the four
winds, from the edge of the world to the edge of the sky.

Then he makes one of the most extraordinary statements in the
Gospels:

> *I tell you truly that this present generation will not be gone until all*
> *these things happen... But no one knows about that day or hour —*
> *not the angels, not God's son, but only God himself.*

Kamada So, if the record is genuine, Jesus expected God to intervene
in this way at any moment.

Whitland Yes, and it was pointed out well over a couple of centuries
ago by the German orientalist Hermann Reimarus that this prediction
made by Jesus must be part of an authentic tradition, because by the
time the Gospels were written, it had been proved to be false, and the
Gospel writers, so far from having any motive to invent it, would have
had good reason to suppress it.

Kamada The whole idea of a God who intervenes is extremely strange
to me. But here is heavenly intervention of a sort — it's beginning to
rain, and we must take ourselves and this recording machine indoors!

Chapter 11

◌

Was Jesus insane?

Kamada As I listen to you, and as I read the Gospels, it becomes clear to me that Jesus was a child of his time. From my professional point of view, I would say that much of what he says is culturally determined. He accepts, as you told me the last time we met, contemporary Jewish ideas about the inauguration of God's reign on earth, and he also comes to accept the belief of people he meets that he is the long-awaited deliverer of Israel.

Whitland I would agree with what you say, but with one proviso. In Jesus' time, all sorts of ideas were current about the expected new age and the saviour of the Jewish people. So there was no agreed, well-defined vision of the new epoch or of the saviour, the man consecrated with the application of olive oil, the anointed one that the Jews called *Mashiah* in Hebrew and *Christos* in Greek — Greek being the first language of most Jews living outside Palestine, among whom most of the early converts to Christianity were to be found.

A modern historian of the Jews, Salo Wittmayer Baron, has said that there were endless variations of the messianic theme. But I suppose that most Jews of Jesus' time imagined the *Mashiah*, the Messiah, as a victorious leader of an army, and most believed that his arrival on the scene was imminent.

Kamada Jesus seems reluctant to call himself the anointed one until the very end of his life, although a very different picture of him in this respect is presented by John's Gospel. Yet it is obvious that he made an extraordinary impression on people, and you have quoted Mark, I believe it was, saying that Jesus' own family thought he was out of his mind.

Whitland That is what Mark says. The word he uses is at the root of the English word 'ecstasy'. This was too much for Matthew and Luke, however, who airbrush this reference to madness out of their own accounts of the incident. But this is not the only reference in the Gospels to Jesus' supposed madness.

On another occasion, according to John, many Jews who heard Jesus claim to be the good shepherd said he was possessed by a demon and was raving mad: John uses a strong word that is related to the English word 'maniac'. In another chapter of John's Gospel, some Jews ask Jesus if he is not a Samaritan — a blameworthy outsider, in their eyes — possessed by a demon.

Kamada If Jesus was alive today, no doubt most people would write him off as insane. But what he did and said — or what the Gospels claim he did and said — surely fitted into most of his contemporaries' picture of the world.

Whitland Yet some modern readers have also got the impression that Jesus was insane, even when they take the common beliefs of his time into consideration. They are troubled, for instance, by the fact that one minute he preaches love and forgiveness, and the next, eternal damnation and torment, sometimes as a punishment for what seem to be relatively minor misdemeanours, and on one occasion for other people's crimes.

It would not be difficult to find other glaring contradictions in Jesus' sayings. He thinks the world will come to an end at any minute, but founds a church.

Kamada It's also strange to turn up at a wedding and celebrate it with a spectacular miracle, if you think the end of the age is imminent.

Whitland Yes, and as we have seen, he insists on the sacredness of the marriage tie, and repeats the Old Testament commandment to honour your father and mother, but excludes the ordinary physical family from his scheme of things.

Jesus says, 'Blessed are those who make peace', but he also says, 'Do not think I have come to bring peace on earth. I have come not to bring peace, but a sabre!'

He gives his followers the impossible command to be perfect, 'just as your heavenly father is perfect'; but he also claims that his yoke is easy and his burden is light, and that only God is good.

In John's Gospel, he says that he has been sent by God to save the world, not to judge it; but in the same Gospel he claims that God has entrusted all judgement to him. And elsewhere in John, in one chapter Jesus says plainly, 'If I am a witness on my own behalf, my testimony is not true', and in another, 'If I am a witness on my own behalf, my testimony is true'. What is one to make of all this?

Kamada There's no doubt one must be a professional Christian theologian to make sense of these remarks.

Whitland One answer to the questions raised by these contradictions and inconsistencies is that they simply confirm the essentially human character of Jesus, for it is part of human nature to entertain contradictory notions and even contradictory ideals. Another explanation might be that Jesus did not say half these things, and that his disciples and the Gospel writers had only a rather dim understanding of what he was about.

But a more sophisticated theologian's argument — or claim, at least — is that being both God and man, Jesus is 'the absolute paradox', and that there is no point in thinking or speaking about him in terms of logic.

'Belief alone can comprehend the paradox,' says one Christian writer, 'an attitude that will risk an experiment in living... Christian faith is something to be lived; it cannot be comprehended *in abstracto*.'

Kamada I am far from wishing to say the last word on such a difficult subject, but one problem I have with this argument is that I cannot will myself either to believe or not to believe a proposition, or a set of propositions. If I understand what is meant by 'belief' in this context, I am inclined to say that I do not find such belief to be volitional.

Chapter 12

Threats and curses in the Gospels

Kamada I am discovering that the Gospels contain many promises. There are many, for example, in the sermon Jesus preached on a mountain: gentle people will inherit the earth; mourners will be comforted; the hungry fed, and so on. But the Gospels also abound in dire curses and terrible threats of eternal fire, of being flung into the outer darkness, of wailing and gnashing of teeth, of worms that never cease to gnaw, of hunger, of mourning, of being cut to pieces, of torture — I think I have said enough.

Whitland One of the strangest threats, which Jesus utters in explaining a parable to his disciples, concerns the fate of slaves who have failed to prepare adequately for the return of their master from a wedding feast. Jesus tells his disciples:

> *The slave who knew what his master wanted, but who has not got things ready or done anything in accordance with his wishes, will be flogged with many strokes of the lash. The slave who did not know what his master wanted, but did things that deserved the lash, will be flogged with fewer strokes.*

Is there anything comparable in the Buddhist scriptures?

Kamada I think not. It is remarkable, too, that in the Gospels, Jesus apparently accepts the legal validity of slavery.

Whitland It is certainly part of his picture of the world, and even if he once made an enigmatic remark about a pupil becoming like his teacher, and a slave becoming like his master, he does not propose the abolition of slavery as an institution.

Kamada Perhaps this also shows that he was not drawing up a scheme for social reform.

Whitland He was no egalitarian, either. Even in the Kingdom of God there is, according to him, a pecking order — a different one from the one we experience in this world, but a pecking order, nevertheless.

But I find it strange that Christian writers on the Gospels rarely seem to comment on these verses in Luke that I have just quoted. I think that if anyone nowadays dwelt in this manner on the nuances of punishment by flogging, we would suspect a morbid interest in the subject.

So to my mind, these verses call for some kind of explanation, but the only direct reference to them that I have come across in modern interpretations of the Gospels is a remark by a Franciscan friar to the effect that 'the punishments for unfaithful and negligent church officials are stark.'

Kamada A Fran-sis-kan? *Mo ichido itte kudasai!*

Whitland A Christian monk belonging to an order founded by the Italian thirteenth-century saint, Francis of Assisi, who preached humility and reverence for all creation.

In spite of this learned monk's special pleading, however, the treatment meted out in the parable to an ignorant slave seems, to say the least, arbitrary. But a threat of punishment which is, ethically speaking, even more shocking is Jesus' promise to the lawyers and synagogue Jews in his audience that they will be held responsible for every murder of a just man committed in the past.

In the course of cursing these Jews seven times, Jesus tells them that all these past crimes will be treated as theirs, from the slaying of Abel (the son of Adam and Eve, who was murdered by his brother Cain) to that of Zechariah son of Barachiah 'whom you' he tells them 'murdered between the sanctuary and the altar'. The Zechariah in question was actually stoned to death on the orders of King Joash of Israel in the year 784 before the Christian era.

Biblical commentators seem to take the enormity of this threat in their ethical stride. I particularly like this blithe comment from the erudite Dr G. B. Caird, an interpreter of Luke's Gospel: 'The present generation must either break with the past by a thorough-going repentance or pay the penalty for the accumulated guilt of past generations.'

Kamada One must be a Christian theologian to find such a statement valid. I myself cannot easily reconcile this threat of punishment for someone else's crimes with my understanding of the Christian notion of the individual human soul, freshly created in each instance as a unique and substantive entity. But are you saying that commentators do not find it objectionable?

Whitland I have not yet come across any objections to it. But in their book, *The Riddle of the New Testament*, the two authors actually applaud this particular threat. They write: 'Here is no ethical idealism, but an urgent moral realism' — whatever that may mean!

And some present-day church leaders certainly seem to accept the notion of present guilt incurred by the past wrongdoing of other people as ethically sound. According to a recent newspaper report, the Rev Stephen Lyas, the Churches Millennium Officer, associated himself with a plea to Christians 'to apologise for the Crusades, slavery, colonialism, and other "past evils", as part of official plans by the major Churches to celebrate the millennium.'

It was also reported that Father Robert Plourde, a Catholic priest and a member of Churches Together in England, said Pope John Paul II had emphasised the need for penitence for past events, which could include the persecution of Protestants by Mary Tudor and of Catholics by Elizabeth I.

Kamada I am not myself celebrating this particular millennium, which may be just as well, because this notion of apologising or being penitent for crimes committed centuries ago by someone else is unintelligible to me.

Whitland This idea stems ultimately from ancient Jewish beliefs. In the Old Testament, God is made to say that he is a jealous God, who attributes the sins of the fathers to their children, their grandchildren, and their great-grandchildren. The notion may have been widespread in ancient times, as the fifth-century BC Greek dramatist Euripides says something to the same effect.

Kamada But this is a primitive belief which should have been discarded long ago. We do not know, and it is unlikely that we ever shall know, whether Jesus said everything put into his mouth in the Gospels, or even more than a small part of what is attributed to him there. But whether he said these things, or the Gospel writers are merely inventing them, this preoccupation with savage punishments calls for explanation.

Whitland It was an extremely cruel age. Four or five years before Jesus was born, the Romans, the ultimate ruling power in Palestine, crucified hundreds, if not a couple of thousand Jewish guerrilla fighters.

There is, I need hardly say, a Freudian explanation of these threats of punishment. As you know, Freud claimed that religious beliefs were not derived from experience or reflection, but were illusions that he described as the fulfilment of the oldest, strongest and most urgent wishes of mankind.

Taking the earliest followers of Jesus to be the masses of the uneducated poor, the proletariat of the Jewish capital city, Jerusalem, and the peasants of the countryside who increasingly felt the urge to change the deplorable conditions in which they lived, the German-American psychologist Erich Fromm argued that these people longed for a happy time for themselves, but also harboured feelings of hatred and dreams of revenge against both the occupying power, the Romans, and the Jewish rulers who were their clients.

This longing and this hatred gave rise, according to Fromm, not only to messianic fantasies of a new age, but to punishment fantasies as well. Fromm advanced this thesis when he was still a strict Freudian, and later on he changed his mind about many of the ideas he put forward in the essay I'm referring to, but without, as far as I know, indicating the detail that he would have liked to revise.

Kamada There is, nevertheless, a distinctly fantastic quality in these threats of punishment in the Gospels.

Whitland Yes, and this is implicitly recognised, to my mind, by some Christian commentators who argue that because some of Jesus' threats are uttered in the context of parables, they are not to be taken literally.

Kamada Yet, if you will allow me to say so, it is one thing to speak in parables — in analogies — and another thing to fantasise.

Whitland I agree. But whatever his frame of mind at the moment in question, Jesus — if Matthew is to be believed — did not recoil from the idea that his heavenly Father would not forgive his creatures, but hand them over to torturers, if they for their part failed to forgive their fellow creatures with all their heart. Again, this threat was uttered as the explanation of a parable about slaves — in this case, a slave whose own debt to his master was cancelled, but who had a fellow-slave who owed him money thrown into prison.

This particular threat by Jesus — 'this is how my heavenly Father will deal with you' — is consistent with the general idea in the Gospels, that just as the greatest joys await those chosen to enter the Kingdom of Heaven, so the worst horrors are reserved for those who will spend the life to come in another place. So, for example, in the famous parable of the rich man in hell and the poor man Lazarus in paradise in Abraham's bosom, the rich man is in torment, and begs Abraham to pity him, and send Lazarus to dip his finger in water 'to cool my tongue, because I am in agony in these flames'.

This parable also dwells on the ugly detail of suffering in this world and suggests that justice is postponed to the next. It also reflects Jesus' belief that our physical bodies are restored in the next world, whether we are in heaven or in hell.

Kamada Of course, the history of the Christian churches shows that many Christians have taken these terrible stories at their face value. And perhaps some still do.

Whitland Yes, in bygone centuries especially, the majority of Christians seem to have taken the idea of hellfire literally, and to their mind this belief justified the burning of other Christians whose views on various doctrinal matters did not coincide exactly with their own. But at the present time, not every Christian takes such an extreme view, although apparently some still do.

In July 1996, a Church of England so-called 'working party' chaired by the Bishop of Newcastle, the Right Reverend Alec Graham, published a report, *The Mystery of Salvation*, rejecting the notion of hellfire and claiming that Hell should be seen as nothingness.

Having 'examined the New Testament closely', the working party discovered that 'there is indeed torment, there is destruction and there is exclusion. Clearly these are not to be understood literally. If they were, they would be contradictory.'

The Times reported that the General Synod 'warmly commended' the working party's conclusions, although some voices were raised in opposition. There were apparently clerics present at the synod meeting at the University of York who were not so keen on giving up the notion of hellfire.

Kamada What do the Gospels say about hellfire in particular?

Whitland Well, what does Jesus himself say on the subject? According to Luke, he told his disciples not to be afraid of those who can merely kill the body, and who have nothing more to do after killing it. 'But I'll show you whom to be afraid of,' he told them. 'Be afraid of him who has the power to throw people into Gehenna. Yes, I tell you, be afraid of him!'

In Jewish traditional belief Gehenna was identified with the valley of fire where, according to the prophet Isaiah, there was 'fire and plenty of wood'. It was an actual place, where children had once been sacrificed by their parents as burnt offerings to Moloch, an ancient local deity.

In Jesus' most famous teaching, the sermon on the mountain that you mentioned earlier, there is another threat of hellfire:

> *Whoever says to his brother 'You moron!' will be answerable for it in the Gehenna of fire.*

The word 'moron' is the actual Greek word in the text, and I suppose most readers of the Gospel would have taken it to mean a dull or stupid person, but some learned men tell us that in Jewish mouths it meant 'renegade'. There are more references to Gehenna in the sermon, and it is made clear that it is a place of real rather than metaphorical fire.

Kamada It must certainly have been real enough to Jesus' immediate audience.

Whitland Yes, and there is yet another collection of fierce threats of hellfire in a famous passage in Mark's Gospel, where Jesus tells his followers:

> *If your hand makes you offend, cut it off: it is good for you to enter into life maimed, rather than to have both hands and go off to Gehenna, into the fire that is never put out. And if your foot makes you offend, cut it off: it is good for you to enter into life lame, rather than to have both feet and be thrown into Gehenna.*
>
> *And if your eye causes you to offend, tear it out: it is good for you to enter the Kingdom of God one-eyed, rather than with both eyes to be thrown into Gehenna, where their worm never dies and the fire is never put out. For everyone will be salted with fire.*

It isn't always obvious what the wrongdoer has done to deserve the harsh punishment meted out to him. In one parable told by Jesus, a king orders a man to be bound hand and foot and thrown into the darkness outside, 'where there will be wailing and gnashing of teeth'. The man's offence is that he has turned up to a royal wedding without wearing a top hat and tails.

The punishment he is given seems a shade severe, but a learned commentator explains that having accepted the wedding invitation, 'the man should have been dressed for the occasion — in other words, good works must go with faith.'

Kamada It seems that theologians can provide an explanation for everything.

Chapter 13

☞

Power fantasies

Kamada We have talked about some promises of a new age and some threats of frightful punishment in a future state that the Gospels attribute to Jesus, and you mentioned that some modern psychologists have interpreted these as fantasies entertained by the oppressed masses of Palestine in New Testament times. What both the threats and the promises seem to me to have in common is a yearning after power.

Whitland One thing is true: the early Christian message was directed to the poor and the oppressed, however much later generations may have modified it, or reconstructed it altogether. But we venture onto notoriously difficult ground if we attempt any psychological analysis of people so remote from us in time and circumstances, especially given the various tendencies and motives of the rather patchy evidence that can properly be cited.

Kamada But before we leave this subject, can we look for a few minutes at the way power is spoken of in the Gospels, as my impression is that power is one of their main themes.

Whitland Are you thinking of power in terms of authority? Then it's true that there are several references to Jesus impressing his audience with the authority with which he preaches. Then the Gospels also say that Jesus claimed the authority to forgive sins, and he exercises this authority on numerous occasions. He also gives his disciples authority to exorcise impure spirits.

Kamada But these are three different forms of authority: the first is intellectual; the second is like a legal authority, a kind of delegated right; and the third is more like an exercise of power, in the sense of a force that is exerted. I am interested in power in this last sense, as something that controls or rules or disposes of other things or other people.

Whitland The same word is used in the Gospels to mean 'authority' in the three instances that you have distinguished. But there is another word, which comes nearer to your notion of power as a source of control. This is *dunamis* in Greek, and it's the source of the English words 'dynamo' and 'dynamic'.

Kamada And 'dynamite', I imagine! We have that word in Japanese, too.

Whitland Well, *dunamis* is a word that can sometimes be translated as 'miracle' in Mark's and Matthew's Gospels, and the link between miracles and power is obvious enough. In fact, when Jesus performs what I think is his only involuntary miracle, the healing of a woman with a persistent haemorrhage, Mark says that he feels that the power has gone out of him, and the word he uses for 'power' is none other than *dunamis*.

Kamada But I was looking for a more general conception of power, something nearer to political power.

Whitland *Dunamis* is used in this sense, too. When Jesus predicts the end of this world, he tells his disciples that after the stars have fallen out of the sky, people will see the Messiah coming in the clouds with great power — *dunamis* — and glory. Even more remarkably, when Jesus is subjected, according to Matthew's account, to a kind of drumhead trial before the Jewish high priest, he refers to himself 'sitting on the right hand of power and arriving on the clouds of heaven'. Here power — *dunamis* again — is equated quite simply with God.

Kamada Power is associated with height... This is interesting, because when Jesus was tempted in the desert by the evil power, this power...

Whitland The Devil.

Kamada Yes, it is a personal being. The Devil, if I remember correctly, sets Jesus on the top of the Temple, and tells him to throw himself down.

Whitland Yes, this is reported in Matthew and Luke.

Kamada I think Jesus was alone, except for the Devil. So this report originates with him. Excuse me, but this fantasy of throwing oneself from a great height and not suffering any harm is a well-known symptom of schizophrenia.

Whitland I am sure there are many symptoms of schizophrenia — and many definitions of schizophrenia, for that matter.

Kamada Another of Jesus' temptations in the desert took place at a height. I am thinking of the high mountain...

Whitland Yes, Matthew says it was a very high mountain.

Kamada And this passage about the clouds that you have just quoted — that is another image of height. Is there any link between these various images of height?

Whitland I do not know of any link.

Kamada Perhaps a psychological link?

Whitland If the Gospels were clinical documents... But I am reminded by what you say of a possible 'height complex' which one scholar has diagnosed, so to speak, in the nineteenth-century German thinker, Nietzsche. Nietzsche was a great enemy of Christianity, of course, but at the same time, understood it more deeply than most Christians.

Kamada In any case, Jesus' temptations in the desert, whether or not one regards them as fantasies, were all to do with power. They were not sexual fantasies. But of course, power and sexuality are closely related.

Whitland Not only when he was tempted in the desert, but in other episodes in the Gospels where Jesus might have been subject to sexual temptation or arousal, there is no mention of anything of the kind, and however closely sexuality and power may be related, they are not the same thing.

Kamada Not exactly, it's true.

Whitland Perhaps I should add that the idea of temptation in the desert is an ancient one. In the Old Testament, the Israelites were led into the desert by their Lord God for forty years, so that this God could humble them, test them, and know their innermost thoughts. The forty years are echoed in the story of Jesus' temptation, as we're told that he spent forty days in the desert. Forty was a ritually significant number throughout south-western Asia in ancient times.

But you are right to raise the question of sexual fantasies in this context. When the first Christian monks took themselves off to the desert for the purpose of abstaining totally and permanently from sexual activity of any kind, they soon began to experience the overwhelming force of sexual urges. There is a striking comment on this by the French scholar, Aline Rousselle. Mlle Rousselle says that the Egyptian saint, Antony, who chose the solitary life late in the third century of the Christian era 'soon discovered that solitude and silence were filled with the amplified voice of man's desires'.

Antony sought to overcome these desires by eating (and then not every day) only bread and salt, and drinking only water, and by going without sleep or any kind of creature comfort. He also shut himself in a tomb, to avoid human contact, but found that so far from eradicating desire, this turned it into a torturing obsession. He was freed, he found, from other struggles, but 'there was only one conflict for him, and that was with fornication'.

During his own sojourn in the desert, Jesus was not subject to this conflict, but that he was aware of sexual imagining, however, is clear from the famous warning in the Sermon on the Mount that if a man looks at a woman with desire, he has already debauched her in his heart.

Chapter 14

☞

Sexual misdemeanours
before Noah

Kamada With Dr Hiraoka's help, I have been following up some of the Gospel statements about the end of this world — if you recall, our discussion of this subject was interrupted by rain. We — Dr Hiraoka and I — have found a passage in Matthew's Gospel where Jesus tells his pupils that the state of affairs when the Kingdom of God is revealed will be similar to what it was in Noah's day, when people were eating and drinking and marrying, and they knew nothing until the flood came and took them all away. The story of Noah is a myth, isn't it?

Whitland Yes, and there were similar myths in other south-west Asian countries that originated at the same time — I suppose about four thousand years ago. Of course, Noah and his ark, as the boat he built to rescue his family is always called, have become a universally known legend in the western world. They were part of the ancient Jews' traditional world picture, and Jesus, too, accepted the story as either symbolically or literally true.

Kamada We need not object to the myth — there is also an ancient Japanese myth about the flooding of the rice fields, although there was no rescue plan, as far as I remember! But the fact that the people at the time of Noah were eating and drinking and marrying seems to be regarded as blameworthy, and Dr Hiraoka is particularly interested in the reference to marrying, and she would be glad if you could explain it.

Whitland Ah, yes — they were eating and drinking and... and what? Well, the next three words in the Greek text have been variously rendered in both modern and earlier translations of the New Testament as 'they married and were given in marriage' or 'they were marrying wives and husbands', and perhaps this is what the ancient texts meant.

Hiraoka Perhaps?

Whitland I mean by 'perhaps' that I'm not sure. In fact, I have more than one objection to these translations. But may I first try to put Noah's story in its biblical context?

You see, according to the Old Testament book of Genesis, the first book in the Bible, in early mythical times, when some fabulous giants called *Nephilim* roamed the earth, ordinary human beings were indulging all the time in evil fantasies. They were so wicked that God was sorry he had created them.

But it was not only human beings who were evil. The whole animal world was also corrupt and violent. So God decided to wipe the whole lot out and start again.

Noah, who was 600 years old at the time, was the only man virtuous enough to be excluded from this wholesale slaughter. So God told him to build a huge wooden boat, with three or four decks, and then take on board his wife and three sons with their wives, and a mating couple of every species of bird, beast and reptile, plus seven mating couples of some specially selected creatures.

Kamada Excuse me — specially selected?

Whitland Yes. These were animals the ancient Jews regarded as clean, and therefore edible. They could eat animals only if they chewed the cud and had divided hooves. Camels were out, for instance, because although they chew the cud, they do not have divided hooves; and pigs were out, because although they have divided hooves, they do not chew the cud.

Kamada That is interesting! There must be a considerable body of anthropological literature on the subject.

Whitland No doubt. But to return to the story in Genesis, the next three chapters describe in picturesque detail how God, by means of a worldwide flood, then blotted out every living thing that was on the face of the ground, human beings and animals and creeping things and birds of the air — they were all annihilated.

But Noah and his family were saved in their great boat, and so were the animals and birds he had taken with him, although some of the best ones were chosen by him to be cooked and offered to God, who liked the smell of the burnt meat.

Oddly enough, once Noah had been saved in this way, it all got too much for him, and he got drunk on some of his own wine — he had planted the world's first vine — and behaved badly. But he lived another 350 years, and the whole population of the earth is descended from his three sons.

Kamada It's a good story. I like the round figures 600 and 350 — it's unusual to find data of that sort in myths. But you were saying that you had some problems with the translation of Jesus' own reference to the state of the world in Noah's day.

Whitland Yes, my first objection to the traditional translations is prompted by the general sense of Jesus' remark, which is not a direct quotation from the book of Genesis, but Jesus' own version of what happened at that time.

The disciples would have known, and Jesus obviously assumes that they would know, that at the time he was talking about — the days leading up to the flood — human beings were supposed to have been misbehaving themselves so badly that God's only recourse was to destroy them. Eating and drinking seem fairly blameless activities, but the suggestion is that people were indulging themselves heedlessly. To my mind, to say in the same context that they were marrying wives and husbands indicates a quite different pattern of behaviour — one that was perfectly proper, lawful, and indeed responsible.

Hiraoka Yes, this is also my difficulty with these words of Jesus. We have seen that in spite of his attack on the natural family, Jesus insisted on the marriage vows. He also, so we are told, celebrated a wedding by turning water into wine for the wedding guests. So I do not think he could have seen 'marrying wives and husbands' as something objectionable.

Whitland I'm glad we agree on that! I only hope that my second difficulty does not strike you as pedantic. It arises from the tense of the Greek verbs: 'they were eating, they were drinking, they were marrying'. This tense in Greek indicates a continuous or habitual activity, something that people indulge in regularly, in other words — just like eating and drinking, in fact. But no one gets married every day, and very few people make a habit of marrying.

Hiraoka I know of no one in Japan who has such a habit, but perhaps in the United States...

Kamada Even there, very few.

Whitland So you see my problem. And my third difficulty is specifically with the second of the two marriage words — the word that is usually translated as 'they were given in marriage'.

Hiraoka I am sure this refers to women!

Whitland Yes. But the exact meaning of this word — or these words, I should say, because Matthew and Luke use different, though closely related, words — the exact meaning is disputed.

Luke uses the passive form of a verb that means, according to the dictionary, 'to give a daughter in marriage'. But in another part of the New Testament, in a strange and difficult passage in one of St Paul's letters, there is dispute between biblical scholars as to whether the same verb does convey anything to do with giving a daughter in marriage, or whether it means simply marrying her, in the sense that her fiancé would marry her.

My own inclination is to interpret these words in the passage about Noah's contemporaries as a description of widespread fornication, rather than habitual marrying. Behaviour of that kind, rather than merely 'taking wives and taking husbands' would have been highly reprehensible in the eyes of the Gospel writers, and even, in their view, likely to dispose God towards wholesale and undiscriminating annihilation of the entire human race.

But I have another reason for reading this meaning into Jesus' description of the fine goings on in the time before Noah. You see, the Greek words in question, from the time of Homer to the present day, have often referred, either implicitly or even explicitly to the sexual act. Indeed, in present-day Greek, they mean only 'to fuck' and 'to be fucked', and I have little doubt that this is the sense that these words in the Gospels would have conveyed to many of the readers for whom they were originally intended.

Exactly what Jesus himself meant on this occasion, however, must remain a matter of conjecture, because he was presumably speaking Aramaic, not Greek. But if he did refer only to taking wives and taking husbands, it is still not possible to say what was so wicked about that.

Chapter 15

☞

Did Jesus have a partner?

Kamada It is usually assumed, isn't it, that whatever his views on marriage, Jesus himself was celibate?

Whitland Yes, although as Susan Haskins so elegantly remarks in her book about Mary Magdalene, 'The New Testament contains no reference to Christ's sexual status.' But apparently some theologians have suggested that he was married, on the grounds that this would have been usual for a Jewish teacher of his age.

Hiraoka Jesus was about thirty when he began to preach and perform miracles?

Whitland Yes, according to Luke. But an authoritative writer, Peter Brown, asserts that, in the eyes of Jesus' contemporaries, there would have been nothing remarkable about his celibacy — it was what they expected of a prophet.

In Jesus' day, too, there were communities of male celibates in Palestine, and in 1947 the library of one of these communities was discovered near Qumran, on the west side of the Dead Sea.

In the 37-volume encyclopaedia that he compiled single-handed about thirty or forty years after Jesus' death, the Roman author Pliny briefly describes such a community — 'the solitary tribe of the Essenes' he calls them. It's interesting that he also locates them on the west side of the Dead Sea. Pliny claimed that this tribe, in spite of not reproducing, had persisted for thousands of ages by continual recruitment of new adherents whose qualification for membership was that they were tired of life.

He calls them 'more astonishing than any other people in the world, without any women, having renounced sexual love, having no money, and only palm-trees as partners'.

Kamada Palm trees as partners!

Whitland That is my rather free translation of Pliny's expression *socia palmarum*. But a Roman wife could be called a *socia* of the marriage bed, and in some southern Italian dialects a derivative of the word is still used to mean 'mistress'.

Hiraoka But there is no suggestion in the Gospels that Jesus had a partner?

Whitland Not in the Gospels. But in 1945, some Egyptian peasants, digging near the town of Nag Hammadi for some soft soil that they used as a natural fertilizer, accidentally uncovered a large earthenware jar. When they smashed it open, hoping to find coins in it, they discovered instead a collection of very ancient leather-bound books. The story of what subsequently became of these books is a complex drama involving a local history teacher, black market dealers in antiquities, a number of scholars of international renown, and Egyptian civil servants.

The books were, in fact, a collection of early Christian texts which, except for some Greek fragments already known from earlier discoveries in Egypt, had been completely lost until the discovery at Nag Hammadi.

Kamada Yes, I have heard of these Nag Hammadi books. I believe they throw new light on some of the religious sects that were early rivals of Christianity.

Whitland And they add to our understanding of early Christianity itself. After all, in addition to the New Testament Gospels, in the first centuries after Jesus' death, many other books about him were written and promoted by rival groups claiming to be his followers. About thirty of these books were apparently published as Gospels. But by the end of the second century, if not a decade or two earlier, they had all been banned by the bishops of the Christian Church — the church that was already calling itself universal.

The books found at Nag Hammadi included four of these banned Gospels, written in the second half of the fourth century in Coptic, a language evolved from ancient Egyptian. But they were translations from earlier Greek texts, and preserved some Greek words which were either loan words commonly adopted by Coptic or words for which the translators found no obvious Coptic equivalent.

One of these unofficial Gospels is the Gospel of Philip, described by one modern scholar as a 'theological treatise, not remotely comparable in form with the New Testament Gospels'. It cannot be dated with certainty, but it may have been written as early as the second half of the second century.

It contains a startling reference to Mary Magdalene who, in the New Testament Gospels, is the most important among the women who followed Jesus in his ministry. This is how a leading scholar, Dr R. McL. Wilson, translates this passage:

There were three who walked with the Lord at all times, Mary his mother and her sister and Magdalene, whom they called his consort. For Mary was his sister and his mother and his consort.

Hiraoka *Sumimasen!* Please explain this Mary who was both his sister and his mother!

Whitland No, all that sentence means is that Jesus' mother and his sister and his consort were all named Mary.

Hiraoka So many Marys again! But please explain what is meant by the word 'consort'?

Whitland This is the word used by Dr Wilson to translate the ancient Greek word *koinonos*, which comes in the original Coptic text. It is a word of several meanings in Greek, most of which — rather curiously, considering the historical and cultural distance between the two languages — can be properly translated into English as the one word 'partner'.

In the New Testament itself, in the Gospels in fact, this word is used by Jesus in the plural in the sense of 'partners in crime'; and Luke uses it to mean 'partners in a fishing business'.

Older Greek writers also used the word *koinonos* in a similar way. This is what Plato calls a bricklayer's mate, and his pupil Aristotle, discussing the exchange of goods in a money-based economy, talks of transactions between equals and partners, resorting to the same word.

Hiraoka We cannot cover so many meanings with one word in Japanese. But in English, you also call a lover 'a partner', don't you?

Whitland Yes, and this meaning is also borne by the word *koinonos*. Plato, for one, particularly likes to use *koinonos*, and the related verb and abstract noun, in a sexual sense.

He says, for example, that a man in love is useless as a partner when it comes to intellectual matters — by partner he means, being Plato, a male lover. In his great dialogue on love, *The Drinks Party*, he uses the word *koinonia* for a partnership between male lovers which, he claims, can give birth to wisdom and virtue — a progeny, he says, that is much better than natural children. But elsewhere, in the context of some way-out laws he dreamt up in his old age for a model city, he uses the verb *koinonei* to refer to illicit sexual intercourse between a man and a woman.

Kamada But languages change over time, and Plato was writing long before this Gospel according to Philip. Can you be sure that the meaning of your Greek word hadn't changed in this period?

Whitland The famous Greek biographer and moral philosopher Plutarch is much nearer in time to the author of this Gospel attributed to Philip, and it can be seen from his essay on sexual love, and in his advice to young married couples, that *koinonos* and the related words were used in the Greek of Jesus' own time and after in the sexual sense. In these books Plutarch also often strikes a curiously modern note — at one point, for instance, he refers to the homosexual male habit of cruising.

There is a passage in the essay on love where Plutarch insists, against the lofty claims of Platonism, that paederasty must involve sexual partnership, and the word he uses is *koinonia*. And in his advice to young marrieds, it is remarked in passing that 'they say no woman ever produced a child without the partnership — *koinonia* again — of a man'.

Kamada What a sensible man this Plutarch evidently was! By that, I hope I mean more than that I agree with him!

Whitland He's a great writer and, after all, Shakespeare found him useful. But what I think Plutarch shows here is that it is quite possible that when the writer of the Gospel of Philip mentions Mary Magdalene as Jesus' *koinonos*, he does mean 'partner' in the modern, sexual sense. Dr Wilson's translation of the word as 'consort' is more dignified, but this is hardly a word in common use nowadays, and certainly not in this sense.

There is also a later passage in the Gospel of Philip that Dr Wilson translates as follows:

> *And the consort of Christ is Mary Magdalene. The Lord loved Mary more than all the disciples, and kissed her on her mouth often. The others too... they said to him 'Why do you love her more than all of us?'*

Hiraoka The Lord is Jesus, of course...

Whitland Yes. Some of the words are missing or illegible in the Coptic text, and Dr Wilson has restored them only tentatively, I think, so that perhaps too much should not be made of Jesus kissing Mary Magdalene on the mouth.

Some commentators on this later Gospel have interpreted the sentence beginning 'the others' to mean that the other male disciples were offended, but one scholar takes 'the others' to mean that it was the other women in Jesus' entourage who were expressing their jealousy.

Hiraoka I hope to hear more from you about these women.

Whitland There is a wonderful book about them by an Italian scholar, Carla Ricci. We must try to get hold of a copy for you.

But before we leave the Gospel of Philip, may I remind you that it was not part of the scriptures recognised by the early Christian Church. It was produced, in fact, by a member of a rival sect belonging to a religious movement that both overlapped with and competed with the established church.

Kamada Ah, yes! I recall something of this sort, but I cannot at this moment remember exactly what this movement was.

Whitland I called it a 'religious movement' because it covered a variety of creeds. But they all claimed to offer their initiates exclusive access to the secrets of the universe. This was achieved by means of special knowledge conveyed in mythological terms matched in the present world only by science fiction about intergalactic adventures. And this knowledge was not only the key to the problem of evil, but the guarantee, too, of salvation.

Kamada *Tozen!* You are talking about the Gnostics, aren't you?

Whitland Yes. And they take their name from the Greek word for 'knowledge'. Until the discovery of the Nag Hammadi texts the Gnostic picture of the world was documented almost exclusively from the writings of the early Christian leaders who attacked it, often virulently, as a heresy.

Gnosticism drew on a number of religious and philosophical traditions — pagan Greek, Iranian, Babylonian, Jewish, and Egyptian among them — but the belief that good and evil have separate, independent origins, that the supreme God is outside the physical universe, and that the world we live in was created at several removes from him by a subordinate but essentially hostile being — these beliefs were common to all the Gnostic sects.

Kamada These are dualistic ideas which occur in one form or another in many religions worldwide.

Whitland The very Gospels themselves are not without traces of dualism. Even in what Christians call the Lord's Prayer — the prayer that Jesus gave as a model to his disciples — there is a contrast between heaven and earth that implies they are separate domains, and there is a reference to 'the Evil One' as a distinct power.

Many scholars take the view that John's Gospel in particular was influenced by Gnosticism. And as for the Gospel of Philip, it has been identified as a production of a sect founded by a poet and philosopher educated at Alexandria who elaborated an extremely complex cosmic scheme in which Jesus was in some way distinguished from Christ, who was, he taught, an 'aeon' — apparently meaning a facet of the primal God's personality.

It is obvious that, apart from its remoteness in time from the Jesus of the New Testament, the Gospel of Philip is encumbered with too much cosmological luggage to be taken seriously as a source for the life of Jesus of Nazareth.

Kamada But please allow me to say that from my point of view, it is not less probable that Jesus kissed Mary Magdalene on the lips than that he turned 120 gallons of water into wine, or fed four or five thousand people with five loaves and two fishes, as the New Testament Gospels tell us he did.

Chapter 16

⁀

Was Jesus homosexual?

Whitland Although — or perhaps because — the New Testament Gospels say nothing outright about Jesus' sexual orientation, some readers of the Gospels, even some Christians, have wondered whether he was homosexual.

In 1967, the Rev. Hugh Montefiore, the vicar of Great Saint Mary's, Cambridge, who eleven years later was to be enthroned as Bishop of Birmingham, was asked to give a lecture on Jesus in Oxford. According to his own account, he wondered what was unusual about Jesus, and he asked himself why Jesus was not married: 'All Jewish boys were supposed to produce a child by the age of twenty.'

Montefiore was born into a well-known Jewish family of Sephardi — Spanish or Portuguese — descent, but was converted to Christianity in his teens after having a vision of a 'figure in white' whom he took to be Jesus. One possibility that he considered in his Oxford lecture was that Jesus was homosexual in orientation. In a newspaper interview in June 1996, however, Montefiore protested that he had 'made it perfectly clear' that Jesus was a celibate, and he added that he had been furious when the BBC quoted him as saying that Jesus was a practising homosexual.

Kamada To my mind, it is strange to raise the question in this way — I mean, to surmise that Jesus was homosexual, but celibate, when the Gospels do not say anything explicit on either of these points. Indeed, the Gospels show Jesus mixing freely with men and women, but do not touch on any sexual relationships, as far as I remember.

Whitland I think that most people picture Jesus as being constantly in the company of his male disciples. He had women followers, but they are kept in the background for most of the time in the Gospels. There is, so to speak, a conspiracy of silence about them. With extraordinary sensitivity, Carla Ricci has explored this silence, and the equally remarkable silence of the commentators, especially on some verses at the beginning of the eighth chapter of Luke's Gospel. I believe I mentioned her book the other day.

Hiraoka Thank you. I have already made a note of it.

Whitland In spite of the Gospels' reticence, there is one passage in John's Gospel that has in all likelihood prompted speculation about Jesus' sexuality.

This is where John describes Jesus' last meal with his disciples, and portrays a scene of what might seem intensely physical intimacy to twentieth-century minds: 'There was reclining on Jesus' bosom one of his disciples, whom Jesus loved'.

In another chapter in John's Gospel, the same disciple is referred to in similar words, but in a way that suggests that Jesus singled him out among the other disciples; and this impression is confirmed by the repetition, near the end of John's Gospel of the phrase 'the disciple whom Jesus loved', who is further defined — in case there should be any question as to whom this meant — as 'the one who reclined at the supper on Jesus' breast'.

One interesting point about these passages is that they indicate a discriminating love, one which springs from a preference for one person over others, which, according to a major work on the subject by a modern theologian, is a contradiction of true Christian love, which is 'spontaneous' and 'unmotivated' — undiscriminating, in fact.

In John's Gospel, too, at the last meal, Jesus predicts his betrayal by Judas Iscariot, and some Freudian analysts have read an erotic meaning into the kiss that Judas gave Jesus in the place called Gethsemane, in order to identify him to the men who had come to arrest him before his trial.

Although a careful reading of John's account of the last meal does not at all support the claim that Judas was 'the disciple reclining on Jesus' bosom whom Jesus loved', this is either asserted or implied by some writers, and, in a further elaboration, that 'the eroticism of the relationship between Jesus and Judas may be understood as a sadistic-masochistic bond in which the deepest erotic act is one of murder and submission to murder.'

Kamada Ah, a *shinju*, perhaps.

Whitland A...?

Kamada In Japanese, that is a suicide pact between lovers.

Whitland Indeed! As it happens, an American psychoanalyst writing about Judas, claims that, 'Killing as love or in the service of love can be demonstrated clinically without too much difficulty.' He goes on to mention 'the well-known Japanese custom, hara-kiri' as an example of 'killing as a friendly act'. He is referring to the suicide's friend, who decapitates him with a single stroke of his sword, after the suicide has disembowelled himself.

But, whether or not this analyst is right about an analogy between Judas and the Japanese suicide's friend, I cannot help thinking that even a Freudian is on slippery ground when he tries to analyse a patient who died nearly two thousand years before he could, so to speak, get him on the couch. Yet there are points in the Gospel text that I should like to mention.

Kamada Please...

Whitland It is the way Jesus addresses Judas, when he responds to the kiss. He calls him, in the Greek of Matthew's Gospel, *Hetaire* — that is the form of the word *hetairos* that was used in addressing someone.

I don't know why, but in every translation of the Gospels into English that I have been able to get hold of, this word is given in this place as 'Friend'. But it hardly means that in Greek. A *hetairos* was a comrade-in-arms in the first place, then sometimes a pupil, a member of one's gang — a crony, in fact. That is not the same as friend, is it?

Kamada Not exactly.

Whitland What I mean is this: friendship may be disinterested, or at least not based on a common material interest of any kind. But the relationship between *hetairoi* is based on just such a common interest.

The corresponding word to *hetairos* in Hebrew — perhaps in Aramaic, too — is *chaber*, which, I'm told, even has a certain left-wing flavour, so that it could be translated as 'comrade' in English. But to my mind, the English word that comes closest in its atmosphere to *hetairos* in this context is the word 'mate', as Londoners sometimes use it — workmen, especially — in addressing one another.

Kamada But that is not mate in the sexual sense.

Whitland Not at all. Yet it is also worth mentioning that the feminine form of *hetairos* in ancient Greek, namely *hetaira*, meant a high-class prostitute.

But there is another thing I should like to mention about Judas' act of betrayal. That is the word used for 'kiss' in this episode. It is a strong form of the word most commonly used — it's the same word that Luke uses to describe the woman who kissed Jesus' feet at the dinner party in the Pharisee's house. So one would be wrong to think of Judas' kiss as a merely formal peck on the cheek.

But before one tries to read any erotic significance into the whole episode, one should bear in mind that recent studies of Judas' role have shown that it belongs to mythology rather than history. To say the least, it is doubtful whether the episode of betrayal by a kiss will bear any weight in any attempt to explore the sexuality of Jesus.

Kamada Yes, the fact that mythology and history are blended with theology throughout the Gospels does seem to create insuperable obstacles to such an attempt.

Whitland But whatever the sources and motives of the Gospel writers, and however questionable their evidence, we have hardly any other evidence about Jesus worthy of consideration. So may I remind you that there are at least two other passages in the Gospels that speak of Jesus' love for a man? The first is in John's Gospel.

When Mary and Martha, the sisters of Lazarus, sent a message to Jesus asking his help, it was, simply, 'Look, Lord, the man you love is ill.' This, again, suggests a discriminating love, because the words are enough, apparently, to identify Lazarus. But the very brevity of the words, and the context, hardly allow us to draw any firm conclusions.

The other passage that I have in mind is in Mark. It describes the rich young landowner who asked Jesus what he must do to win eternal life. Jesus reminded him of the ancient biblical commandments, and then 'looked at him in the face and loved him'. The tense of the Greek verb 'loved' here suggests an action begun in the past, but still having an effect in the present. In some ways 'took a liking to him' would come nearer to the sense of the original, except that the love indicated was stronger than a mere liking.

Kamada 'Looked at him and loved him.' It sounds terse. My impression is that Mark inclines to brevity. There is no enlargement on these words in the other Gospels?

Whitland No. On the contrary. Although Mark states that Jesus loved this young landowner, this love is not mentioned by either Matthew or Luke in their account of the incident.

But before we leave this topic, I should remind you of the passage at the end of John's Gospel, where Jesus asks his disciple Peter three times if he loves him, and Peter answers three times that he does love Jesus — perhaps an ironical reminder of the three times that Peter is reported to have denied that he knew Jesus, while Jesus was being interrogated by the Jewish supreme court in Jerusalem before being handed over to the Roman authorities.

The repetition of the question suggests a demand for attention: 'Do you love me?' also means 'Do you still take notice of what I say?' and that is why, when Peter affirms his love, Jesus commands him: 'Feed my lambs. Feed my sheep.'

One thing that is particularly striking about this exchange between Jesus and Peter is that there is an explicit emphasis on that very element of preferring that has been said to be alien to Christian love, even though there is, at the same time, a curious ambiguity in John's original Greek: the first time Jesus asks Peter, he says: 'Simon, son of John, do you love me more than these?' It is not clear whether this means, 'Do you love me more than you love the other persons present?' or 'Do you love me more than these other persons present love me?'

In none of these references to Jesus' love for men or their love for Jesus, however, is there any suggestion of erotic feeling. The Greek verbs used by the Gospel writers imply affection and regard or (as it is sometimes called) brotherly love, and even when they are used by pagan Greek writers, these words hardly ever refer to sexual love.

Kamada But in English, you use the same word 'love' in both cases — I mean, to express brotherly love and sexual love. This is strange to a Japanese, as we use quite distinct words to express these different feelings.

Whitland Perhaps a more fundamental point, however, than these semantic distinctions is that questions about Jesus' psychological makeup will never be answered, because the only Jesus we know or can ever know is a creation of the Gospel writers, and they were not interested in his psychology.

The question simply did not arise for them, and Jesus himself certainly never talked about such matters. Nor did he leave us an autobiography, or even make any autobiographical remarks, such as the apostle Paul makes, for example.

Chapter 17

☞

The love that dare not
speak its name

Kamada You remarked yesterday that the Gospel writers were not interested in the psychological makeup of Jesus...

Whitland Well, I meant that they do not show the kind of interest that a modern writer probably would — they don't attach any psychological labels to him, because there were no psychological labels available to them.

They do not even attempt to characterise him in everyday terms: they don't say, for example, that he was restless, or impetuous, or even brave, though his actions may suggest such attributes. But they do tell us, or claim to tell us, what he said and did and what he suffered — only occasionally do they venture to describe his feelings or thoughts in a subjective way.

Hiraoka Please give an example.

Whitland One that comes immediately to mind is in the episode known to Christians as the agony in the garden. Before Jesus was arrested and tried, he went to a place called Gethsemane to pray. He took three of his disciples with him and, aware of the suffering that was in store for him, he began to feel dismay and anguish. The word the Gospels — Mark and Matthew — use here seems to have a medical background. Then Jesus tells the disciples that his soul is deeply sad, to the point of death. There is an echo of this cry from the depths in John's Gospel, but I cannot think of any other statement of this kind, any statement by Jesus about his own feelings, in any of the Gospels — certainly Jesus nowhere else speaks of his soul in this way.

Kamada So it would be a mistake to look for any attempt at psychological exploration in the Gospels, and you are particularly excluding questions about Jesus' sexuality?

Whitland Yes. I can only repeat Susan Haskins' remark that the New Testament contains no reference to his sexual status.

Kamada But it is not the case, is it, that the Jesus of the Gospels is unaware of the sex drive?

Whitland No. I think I have already mentioned the saying that a man who looks at a woman with desire has already committed adultery with her in his heart. And this saying is followed immediately by the terrifying advice to tear your own right eye out and fling it away if it causes you to sin, because, as Jesus says, 'It is in your interest to lose a part of your body rather than have your whole body thrown into hell.'

But in their way, the sayings in which Jesus, so to speak, rules out sex are more striking — by ruling it out, he implicitly acknowledges its existence.

Kamada What do you mean by 'rules out sex'?

Whitland Oh, I was thinking about his apparent approval of those who have castrated themselves for the sake of the kingdom of Heaven, and the statement that there are no marriages there.

Kamada Tell me about those statements!

Whitland You must give me time to think about them. But I also want to suggest that in repudiating the blood family, and replacing it, as it were, by a universal family, Jesus is denying sex again — he is denying the family based on a sexual bond. Yet, paradoxically, he treats that bond as indissoluble. It is important, too, that — quoting ancient biblical authority — Jesus recognises this bond only between male and female.

Kamada So, whatever his own sexual inclination, Jesus withheld approval from homosexual bonding! But I find that this insistence on the marriage bond is also a way of restricting sexuality, or at least containing it, so that my general impression that the whole sexual scene is somehow an embarrassment to the Gospel writers is confirmed. I would not say that sexual activity is taboo in the Gospels, but it gets an unfavourable, even a negative treatment doesn't it?

Whitland On those few occasions that it is explicitly referred to, I would agree that it is disparaged. But having said that, I do not doubt that the reason is that the Gospel writers want to insist on the superiority of non-sexual love over sexual love.

Kamada Did they think in those terms — I mean, of superiority? Did they even have in mind any comparison between two phenomena to which you give the name of love, but call one sexual and the other non-sexual? Please allow me to say there is a danger here of judging the matter from a modern, and perhaps even from a western point of view.

Hiraoka Is it a question of something that preoccupies one culture, but not necessarily another?

Whitland You are leading me into deep water here. But my first thought is that we do not have enough evidence to answer such a question satisfactorily. In one way or another, anything we know about the sexual mores of first-century Palestine comes, I think, from more or less sporadic references in the laws laid down by religious leaders. There is no systematic or would-be systematic contemporary inquiry, such as some present-day researchers have claimed to carry out.

Hiraoka No statistics! Perhaps that in itself indicates the degree to which the people of Palestine were or were not preoccupied with this matter.

Whitland Well, I'm willing to grant that there were more things in heaven and earth in those days than are dreamt of in your twentieth-century philosophy.

But I shall have to limit myself to the observation that, whenever the Gospels speak of 'love' they always and exclusively mean non-sexual love.

At the same time, I accept Professor Kamada's point that it is a peculiarity of some western languages, and certainly of ordinary English usage, that the same word,'love' can be used — or I should say is used — to express both these emotions or impulses, both the sexual and the non-sexual.

But in Greek, as you have spotted, they are two distinct things, denoted by two distinct words.

Kamada In Japanese, too. Although we do also have a word, *suki*, that covers many aspects of loving or liking.

Hiraoka In fact, we have many words...

Whitland But whether your Japanese words correspond closely to the two Greek words I just referred to — *eros* and *agape* — would, I'm sure, be far from obvious.

Hiraoka I do not think we should try to match them. But can you explain these Greek words to me?

Whitland Can anyone explain them? I once met an American psychoanalyst in my travels — an orthodox Freudian, by the way — who told me, '"Love" isn't a word, it's an encyclopaedia.'

Kamada But one can always consult an encyclopaedia.

Whitland Yes, if you have one handy. In all modesty, however, I have to say that I am not myself an encyclopaedia, so for the time being, at least, you will have to make do with only a few indications.

Well then, *eros* means 'sexual love' or 'sexual desire'— it's the root, of course, of our English word 'erotic' — and *agape* means non-sexual love.

The Gospels repeat the Old Testament command to love the Lord your God with all your heart, with all your soul, and with all your strength; and the command to love your neighbour as yourself.

Hiraoka We have a special expression in Japanese for 'neighbour love' — *rinjin-ai.*

Whitland In the sermon he preaches on a mountain in Matthew's Gospel, Jesus also tells his audience to love their enemies.

Kamada It is interesting that this love is commanded. In other words, both the Old Testament writers and the authors of the Gospels think of love as something that can be produced voluntarily — by a freely chosen act of will. I cannot say that I think of love, whether it is a word or an encyclopaedia, as subject in this way to volition. But perhaps I am misunderstanding what is meant by 'love' here.

Whitland Both the Old Testament and the Gospels are talking here about *agape*, about non-sexual love, of course. As to the point you make about volition, I suppose one can cultivate a disposition to love by a freely taken decision, even if one cannot order oneself to love somebody on a particular occasion.

Kamada Perhaps. But that would seem to be a rather tame matter — love in a minor key. Is that what these biblical commands mean? The words 'with all your heart, with all your soul' suggest to me a passionate love, however non-sexual it may be.

Whitland I agree, and I do not think that anyone claims it is easy to love God in this way, or to love your neighbour as yourself, or to love your enemies in any way. There is another difficulty about love of this kind — it makes no discrimination.

It was Sigmund Freud who raised this particular difficulty most insistently. In his essay *Civilization and its Discontents*, he denied the authenticity of undiscriminating or universal love, and insisted that to love a person meant to prefer him or her to other persons.

Kamada I should like to have a clear idea about this. Are you saying that Freud insisted on the discriminatory nature of love, even of non-sexual love...

Whitland ... which he calls 'aim-inhibited'. Yes. According to him, a love that does not discriminate is thereby deprived of some of its worth.

Kamada Is this aim-inhibited love the same as *agape*?

Whitland Perhaps it is nearer to 'affection' — and the Greeks have a word for that, too. Freud wrote in German, of course, and German also normally translates both *agape* and *eros* by one and the same word. Freud, incidentally, maintains that what he calls 'steadfast, affectionate feeling' — corresponding fairly well to *agape* — is nevertheless derived from what he calls 'genital love' — corresponding to *eros*. This prompts him to say that the careless way in which language (he means the German language, but this applies to English as well) uses the word 'love' has its genetic justification.

Kamada You have said that when the Gospels speak of love, they invariably mean non-sexual love — *agape*. Does this mean that *eros* is never mentioned?

Whitland Not once.

Kamada So perhaps, after all, it is a taboo word for the Gospel writers.

Whitland Perhaps. One reason for the banishing of *eros* from the Gospels that has occurred to me is this: *eros* was not simply a word denoting a state of mind or a state of heart. To many people in the eastern Mediterranean at that time he was a god. I know you have visited London, so you must have been to Piccadilly Circus.

Kamada Yes, of course.

Whitland Then you have seen Alfred Gilbert's statue of the god Eros, poised on his Art-Nouveau pedestal.

Hiraoka He is a young god.

Whitland At the drinks party described by the Greek philosopher

Plato, one of the guests says Eros is the oldest god, while another says he is the youngest.

Eros seems, in fact, to have arrived comparatively late on the Greek scene. He was never the object of worship throughout the whole of Greece, let alone the Greek-speaking world, but wherever his cult was established, he retained this divine or semi-divine status until well into the Christian era — I say 'semi-divine' because this is how Socrates' mysterious teacher, Diotima, describes him in Plato's dialogue.

She says that Eros is not a god, but a great demon, something between god and mortal, and indeed an intermediary between them, conveying prayers and sacrifices from men to the gods, and commands and rewards for sacrifices from gods to men.

Kamada Was that the general view of the god Eros, do you suppose?

Whitland Do you mean, was that the view of the man in the Greek street — the charcoal-burner worried by law-suits, depicted in Greek comedy? I think that very little is known about his religious beliefs or feelings. We have to wait for Christianity to enter the Greek world before we can say anything much about personal religious experience.

Kamada But whatever the standing or power of this god or demigod Eros, it was too much for the authors of the Gospels.

Whitland Yes, that would certainly be one way of putting it. The sexual love that Eros represents is the love that dare not speak its name in the Gospels.

Chapter 18

꩜

Sexual love and death

Kamada Miss Hiraoka has asked me to remind you that the last time we met, you quoted the Gospels as saying that there are no marriages in the kingdom of Heaven. We should both like to hear more about that.

Whitland Yes, and if I remember rightly, I asked for time to look into that. Well, I have looked at this saying in its Gospel context, and I must begin by explaining that the Jews of Jesus' time were divided on the matter of life after death.

The Jews most closely associated with the local town and village religious meeting-houses, the synagogues, believed in the immortality of the individual person and in physical, bodily resurrection. But the wealthier Jews associated more closely with the Temple in Jerusalem and the high-ranking priests who officiated there denied that — as the Gospels put it — dead bodies could stand up again. They believed that human beings' personal existence was confined to the here and now.

It was, the Gospels say, some Jews of this latter class who came to Jesus one day and tried to put him on the spot by putting a trick question to him.

Hiraoka Excuse me. To put him on the spot?

Whitland I mean to put him in an awkward predicament. They must have known, you see, that Jesus himself did believe in bodily resurrection. So, in order to ask him what they thought would be an unanswerable question, they invented a rigmarole about seven brothers.

The first hypothetical brother in their conundrum marries, but dies childless. The second brother then marries his widow (in accordance with Jewish law), but also dies childless. He is followed by the third brother, with the process repeating itself until all seven brothers have married the same woman, all of them failing to father a child.

Finally, the woman herself dies, and here comes the snide question put by these upper class Jews to Jesus: 'When the dead rise again, whose wife will she be? Because the seven of them had her as their wife.'

'When people rise from the dead,' Jesus replies, 'they neither marry, nor are they given in marriage, but are like angels in the heavens.'

Hiraoka So his audience had clear and firm ideas about these angels!

Kamada But I am interested in this: at first sight this reply rules out marriage for the people in question, but does it necessarily rule out sexual intercourse? Perhaps there is free love in the afterlife, even if there are no marriages.

Whitland There are versions of this episode in all three narrative Gospels. But Luke makes it explicitly clear that the meaning of Jesus' reply is that there is no sexual intercourse between the risen dead. Here is how Luke reports Jesus' words:

> *The children of this age marry and are given in marriage. But the people who have been judged worthy to win a part in that age and to rise up from the dead neither marry nor are given in marriage, because they can no longer die. Because they are like angels, and they are the children of God, being, as they are, children of the resurrection.*

Now, a learned modern commentator on Luke remarks that Jesus did not hold the naïve view of resurrection these Jews (by implication) attributed to him when they put the question of the seven brothers to him. He says: 'Jesus had simply to state, therefore, that in an existence which has no place for death, marriage as a means of propagating the species or assuring a legal succession becomes irrelevant.'

Kamada Yes, I can see that 'marriage as a means of propagating the species' certainly implies sexual intercourse.

Whitland So this commentator supports the interpretation that sexual intercourse is what Jesus is ruling out 'in that age' — which means in that future state when the resurrection of 'those judged worthy' takes place.

A few days ago, we talked about the bad behaviour of the human race in the days before the flood. You may remember that I found it puzzling that marrying wives and husbands was cited as something that incurred the wrath of God and invited destruction.

Kamada I believe you put a particular interpretation on the Greek words...

Hiraoka Yes, the words 'married and given in marriage'.

Whitland Now, in this confrontation with the upper class Jews, in Luke's account of it, Jesus uses the same words. But one of them is in a slightly different grammatical form — one that is linked to a verbal form used by some ancient Greek authors to emphasise repeated or habitual actions.

And I am suggesting that these words make better sense if they are taken to imply, at least, what they nowadays mean in Greek, where they refer simply to that act, the importance and dignity of which is the subject of a pleasingly ironic comment by the eighteenth-century Scottish philosopher David Hume.

Kamada I believe I understand you.

Whitland Perhaps my immoderate interest in Greek is leading me to put immoderate language into Jesus' mouth. But in any case, whether Jesus implied the f— word or meant to express himself in (to modern tastes) more moderate language is not as interesting as the link that, according to Luke, he makes between sexuality and mortality.

Hiraoka Mortality?

Whitland Death. Let me remind you of Luke's actual words: 'They neither marry nor are given in marriage, because they can no longer die.' One of the early leaders of the Greek Orthodox Church, St John Chrysostom, himself a 'fervent upholder of the virtue of sexual asceticism', spelt this out more plainly in his famous sermon on virginity.

Explaining to his congregation in Constantinople that Adam and Eve's disobedience, as reported in the Old Testament, cost them 'the happy life, beauty and the honour of virginity', he insisted that, 'Where there is death, there too is sexual coupling; and where there is no death, there is no sexual coupling either.'

But there is an even stranger, and in a way deeper, linking of sexuality and death in the unofficial second-century Gospel of Philip — the Gospel, if you recall, that claims that Mary Magdalene was Jesus' partner. This writer does not link death to the primeval couple's disobedience, but to the separation of the sexes: 'When Eve was in Adam, there was no death; but when she was separated from him, death came into being. Again if she goes in, and he takes her to himself, death will no longer exist.'

Kamada That is a remarkable statement. If I have understood it, it implies that death is the price we pay for our sexual nature. It is a kind of biological insight.

Whitland Yes, and I gather that the latest scientific thinking on this subject is that it is indeed the imperatives of sexual reproduction that condemn us to dusty death.

Kamada There is also a psychological link...

Whitland Well, Freud wrote about an instinct of death or destruction, opposed to, but closely linked with what he called 'libido', which in turn he sometimes seemed to equate with *eros*. He even went as far as to claim that all life consisted essentially of the struggle between *eros* and death.

Kamada So, it is not only theologians who reach out after statements of maximum content!

Whitland It is striking how much of Freud's writing is purely speculative. But on this point he is heir to an age-old tradition. There is a fragment of the ancient Greek dramatist Sophocles that explicitly links death and *eros* — 'now that he is dead, I am seized by desire (*eros*) to die with him' — and I'm sure there are many similar lines of poetry that could be quoted.

And not only poetry. You know that I have been reading Yukio Mishima's novels lately and, wait a moment — yes, I've got it here. What about this, from *The Sailor Who Fell from Grace with the Sea*, in John Nathan's translation:

> *For Ryuji the kiss was death, the very death in love he always*
> *dreamed of... in the dark rapture of all this was something directly*

linked to death. He was perfectly aware that he would leave her in a day, yet he was ready to die happily for her sake. Death roused inside him, stirred.

Kamada It seems that Mishima was obsessed by the idea of a beautiful death, and this led him, some people think, to commit hara-kiri as a supreme sexual act. It has also been suggested that he and his lover committed a double suicide for love — a *shinju*, in Japanese. But here again, we have entered the realm of speculation.

Whitland That reminds me of our discussion of Judas Iscariot, and the interpretation of his relationship to Jesus that some Freudian analysts have suggested. I'm sure we could pursue this theme of *eros* and death much further in literature and art: think of Romeo's 'Thus with a kiss I die' and Juliet's last words in Shakespeare's play — one does not have to be a Freudian to feel their Freudian significance.

And as we go in to supper, perhaps you will allow me to remind you of Wagner's idea of the supreme bliss of love in death that is the climax of Isolde's ecstatic song.

126

Chapter 19

Jesus recommends self-castration

Kamada The last time we met, you quoted a saying that Luke, in his Gospel, attributes to Jesus, to the effect that there is no sexual coupling in the next world. The link between death and the sexual impulse led us far from the Gospels, however. But what Dr Hiraoka and I would like to know, is whether you have anything further to say about the undervaluation of the sexual impulse in the Gospels.

Whitland Undervaluation! That is one way of putting it. Luke likened the risen dead to the angels of ancient Jewish belief. But in Matthew's Gospel there is a far more fierce saying that presents the same point of view — the assertion that there is no sexual activity in the kingdom of heaven.

Jesus has just told his disciples that a man may not divorce his wife (Jewish law allowed only a husband, not a wife, to divorce) and marry another, except in one particular case. The disciples say: 'If that is how it is between husband and wife, it's not worth getting married.'

Jesus' reply to this is strange: 'Not everyone can accept what I am going to say, but only those who have had it granted to them. For there are eunuchs who were born like that from their mother's womb; and there are eunuchs who were castrated by men; and there are eunuchs who castrated themselves for the sake of the kingdom of the heavens. Let anyone accept this who can.'

Kamada He actually uses the word 'eunuch'? Such a man was known in the world of Jesus?

Whitland Oh, yes. Eunuchs are mentioned in books of the ancient Jewish scriptures that were well known to the writers of the Gospels.

In the Old Testament story of the ninth-century king of Israel, Jehu, we are told that when he arrived on horseback in Jerusalem, two eunuchs appeared at the palace upper windows, and on Jehu's orders, threw the Phoenician princess Jezebel down to be trampled to death by the king's horse.

Elsewhere in the Old Testament, eunuchs are mentioned favourably. A fifth-century prophet says no eunuch should regard himself as a dry stick. According to this prophet, God says that eunuchs who observe his Sabbaths and do what God wants will be given a monument and a name in God's house that are 'better than sons and daughters'.

But to return to Matthew's Gospel, the Greek word *eunouchoi* in these two verses is, of course, the source of our own word 'eunuch', and it meant originally a man who could be trusted to look after a royal bedchamber, because he had been castrated. From it a verb has been derived, which means quite simply 'to castrate'.

As far as I have been able to check, all modern translators of the Gospels into English seek to tone down the Greek, which I have just translated literally. The *New English Bible* even goes so far as to translate 'eunuchs' as ' (those) incapable of marriage', which on any reading would surely denote a far larger category of men than eunuchs.

Kamada Yes, that must be so.

Whitland Even *The New Jerusalem Bible*, which is usually so close to the original Greek, avoids using the word 'castrate', and restricts its interpretation of the passage to a prim footnote: 'Christ invites to per-

petual continence as an expression of total consecration to the kingdom of God.'

If this, or something like it, is what Jesus meant, one is still left wondering what he meant by 'eunuchs who were castrated by men' which
does not make sense if we assume that he is using the word 'castrated'
in a peculiar metaphorical or symbolic sense.

In any case, whatever modern commentators make of this saying,
there is no doubt that many early Christians took it literally, and some
of them even put Jesus' implicit advice into effect.

Kamada Do you mean that they physically castrated themselves?

Whitland Yes, or voluntarily invited a doctor to do the job for them.
The most famous of these self-mutilators was the brilliant
Alexandrian biblical scholar Origen, the first Christian, so it has been
said, to be 'a genuinely philosophical theologian'. His life straddled the
first and second centuries of the Christian era. Although he was not
quite so precocious as some American child evangelists, he became an
exponent of the Christian scriptures while still a teenager.

His ideas about human personality and the universe in which it
functions and develops show that he would have had little difficulty
with modern notions of the subconscious, and would have enjoyed
some works of science fiction.

But he had strange notions about human sexuality and 'other
seemingly indestructible attributes of the person associated with the
physical body', which, as Peter Brown puts it in his masterly book on
the body and society in those times, 'struck him as no more than provisional'.

Hiraoka Provisional?

Kamada *Zanteiteki na...* You call it a strange notion, but it is an interesting one. My inclination would be to ask what is meant by 'the person', but that would lead us too far away from our present topic.

Whitland But one day, perhaps...

I certainly do not wish to attribute what Americans call 'a mindset' to Origen. But it does seem to have been his personal view of the human body as 'always a limit and a source of frustration' that led Origen to the doctor to get himself castrated. Such, at any rate, is the story related more than a century later by Eusebius, the bishop of Caesarea, the Palestinian port where Origen died in the local prison after being tortured for his religious beliefs.

Eusebius had access to the church library at Caesarea that Origen himself had put together, and although a modern scholar has doubted his story, it may well be true. Eusebius tells us that Origen underwent the operation to scotch rumours that he had physical relationships with some of the young women in his spiritual care, and adds, by the way, that Origen later bitterly regretted the operation. Perhaps he came to the view that the Gospel endorsement of self-castration was not, after all, to be taken literally, and this may have prompted his later idea that the Bible in general was susceptible of interpretation as allegory.

Kamada He paid a heavy price for this conclusion.

Whitland Indeed! But whether or not Eusebius' account of Origen's castration is true, many third- and fourth-century Christians had no difficulty in believing it, because self-castration was quite a common practice at that time. According to Peter Brown, 'The very matter-of-fact manner in which monastic sources report bloody, botched attempts at self-castration by desperate monks shocks us by its lack of surprise.'

Instances of self-mutilation are attested in the early history of the

Christian church, and it was even found necessary to draw up rules against it. In the third century, the learned Roman priest Hippolytus barred from Holy Communion, among others, 'all homosexuals and those who had emasculated themselves.'

A fourth-century collection of regulations, based on decisions of older Eastern church councils, forbids a man who mutilates himself to become a cleric 'because he is a self-murderer and an enemy of God's creation'. Another rule excommunicates for three years any layman who mutilates himself 'because he has designs on his own life'. Those who drew up these rules could certainly have cited Old Testament authority, as the code of civil and religious laws known as Deuteronomy expressly excludes from the assembly of the Lord any-one whose testicles have been crushed or whose penis has been cut off. In spite of these weighty authorities, however, we still hear of an act of self-castration in Byzantium as late as the sixth century.

Kamada So however strange Origen's ideas may have been, they were shared by other early Christians. There must have been some cultural factors at work.

Whitland You mean, of course, the anthropological sense of 'cultural'. I am not an anthropologist, but I could say something about the historical background, perhaps.

Kamada Please do.

Whitland Eunuchs appear in western history I think for the first time in Egypt in the eleventh century BC, but it has been supposed that there were earlier precedents in the part of the world now known as Iraq. But it was in the Persian empire five or six centuries before the Christian era that eunuchs played an important role, and established a tradition that was carried on for centuries in the eastern Christian empire.

131

We are spared the details of how these courtier eunuchs lost their manhood, although the Greek historian Herodotus tells a horrible story of a Greek from the island of Chios who kidnapped young boys, castrated them, and sold them to the Persians.

In Matthew's Gospel, as I quoted, Jesus talks of 'eunuchs who were castrated by men' and he distinguishes these eunuchs from those who are the point of his remark, who were the 'eunuchs who castrated themselves for the sake of the kingdom of the heavens'.

Although this is the literal meaning of Matthew's Greek, Jesus himself — if indeed the saying is authentic — may have meant to speak symbolically in the latter part of this saying, and simply talking of 'chaste abstinence' or voluntary celibacy, 'the cost', as one modern commentator puts it, 'of a life dedicated to the service of God, as in our Lord's own case'.

Kamada But if all modern commentators take the words in this sense, why did Origen and other early Christians apparently take the words literally? And even where there is a tradition of eunuchs, the practice of self-castration calls for explanation.

Whitland I agree. And it is curious that Origen himself did not always take the sacred scriptures literally. In fact, in one of his books he goes out of his way to explain that the scriptures have various levels of meaning, literal, moral and spiritual.

But there was a tradition of self-castration in some pagan cults in the eastern Mediterranean, notably that of the great mother goddess Cybele in Phrygia — an area in what is now Turkey. Cybele's eunuch priests, known as Galli, 'dashed the severed portions of themselves against the image of the cruel goddess' and then 'reverently wrapped them up and buried them in the earth as instruments of fertility', before dressing in women's clothes.

These eunuch priests were commemorating the self-mutilation of the mother goddess's lover, Attis, an Asiatic fertility god of Semitic origin. There was a spring festival of death and resurrection dedicated to him.

Kamada Yes, there was more than one cult of this type... and they have inevitably been compared with Christian belief.

Whitland Of course. But Attis also corresponded in some aspects to the Phoenician god Baal, whose worship Jezebel — the princess trampled to death by Jehu's horses — had introduced into Israel from her birthplace, Sidon.

The cult of the Great Mother goddess Cybele was brought to Rome in the year 204 before the Christian era, and was confused with the cult of the earth goddess Rhea. In the next century it exerted a powerful impact on the imagination of Latin poets.

So Catullus, for example, who was born about 80 years before Jesus, describes Attis 'tearing away the weight from his loins with a sharp flint'. In the same poem, Attis calls on the eunuch priests by a female name, and tells them they have emasculated themselves out of exaggerated hatred of Venus, the goddess of love.

When Attis has castrated himself, Catullus calls him a 'spurious woman' and represents him as bitterly regretting his action. Catullus ends this great poem with a prayer to Cybele: 'make other men excited, make other men mad' (but not me!).

Attis' fame lingered in Rome at least as late as the third century of the Christian era. There, the teacher Hippolytus that I mentioned just now claimed, in his massive *Refutation of All Heresies*, that Attis was raised to 'the celestial essence where, they say, there is neither female nor male, but a new creation, a new man, who is androgynous'.

Another opponent of heresy, Tertullian, was actually converted to Christianity towards the end of the second century after seeing a condemned Christian, dressed by Roman soldiers to look like Attis, torn apart alive in a north African arena.

Chapter 20

☞

Jesus and women's rights

Kamada It would go beyond the evidence, perhaps, to say that sex matters in general were a taboo subject in Jesus' circle. But the sayings attributed to him in the Gospels that you have quoted certainly suggest strong disapproval of the sexual act.

Dr Hiraoka wishes to ask whether this bias in the Gospels is related to a general hostility to women.

Whitland I do not think so. Several modern writers have stressed the fact that in the Gospels, after Jesus has risen from death, he reveals himself first to women — not to his male disciples.

But one has to consider this question of how far there may be bias against women in the Gospels in the more general context of the status of women in Palestine in the first century of the Christian era.

Naturally, a great deal has been written on this topic, especially in the last 50 years, and it is dangerous to generalise. But one contemporary authority on the subject, Ben Witherington — who is the third in succession in his family to be so named — says that although the religious leaders among the Jews of Jesus' time held a variety of opinions about women and their roles, their assessment was predominantly negative.

Witherington goes on to say, however, that Jesus 'not only countered these negative evaluations, but also endorsed and extended women's rights beyond any positive evaluations' that some people may have had at the time.

Hiraoka *Sumimasen!* Endorsed women's rights?

Whitland Witherington means that Jesus supported women's rights, and sought to enlarge them. But I am bound to say that when we are trying to discuss social matters in Palestine or any other place during the first century of the Christian era, we should be wary of the notion of 'women's rights' that Mr Witherington has introduced here. In this context we should not even speak of 'men's rights', even if men at that time and in that place generally regarded women as subordinate to them.

Kamada Do you mean that no one had any rights at that time?

Whitland Well, rights of a kind were recognised in the ancient Mediterranean world, but always, I think, in a legal context. There could be a right to property, for example, or a right to have a contract honoured. But there were no general rights, still less general rights that could be attributed to women rather than to men, or in distinction from men.

Kamada When you say 'rights', you are thinking of claims — claims to such things as proper medical treatment or to opportunities for useful employment?

Whitland Yes, rights in this sense would often mean claims. As you know, the American Declaration of Independence asserted in 1776 that all men are created equal and are endowed by their Creator with certain unalienable rights, including the right 'to pursue happiness'.

Kamada The Anglo-Saxon notion of happiness seems ill-defined to me. I cannot understand it in terms of a claim.

Whitland No, but my point is that until the eighteenth century, hardly anyone would have had much idea of what was meant by rights of the kind envisaged by the authors of the American Declaration of Independence.

That Declaration, by the way, makes no mention of women — it refers only to men, although I suppose that meant mankind, and was understood to include women.

As for some later reaffirmations of the American ideal, such as the 1948 United Nations Universal Declaration of Human Rights, they invoke an ideal of equality that is absent from Jesus' teaching.

But in challenging Ben Witherington's argument, I would not wish to suggest that Jesus went along with the general tendency of his time to regard women as somehow inferior to men. It is true that his account of God is couched in exclusively masculine terms, and his disciples are usually thought of as being only men, but according to Luke he was also accompanied on his travels by a number of women, some of whom helped to pay his expenses.

As far as I can tell, this was the first time in history that Jewesses in Palestine left home to accompany a travelling preacher — at least, it is the first record of such a thing. It is also surprising to me that the Gospels — Luke, that is — makes only a passing reference to such a remarkable, not to say provocative, innovation on the part of Jesus, especially as some of the women were very probably social outcasts.

Hiraoka But I still do not understand. These women, you say, accompanied Jesus, and they helped to support him. But were they his students, his...

Whitland You mean, his disciples...

Hiraoka Yes, I mean in the same way that the men were. Excuse me a moment... [*She confers in Japanese with Professor Kamada.*]

Kamada Yes. We believe there is a dispute among Christians as to whether women may be appointed priests. Dr Hiraoka wonders whether Jesus appointed any of these women.

Whitland Ordained them — made them priests? No. He certainly could not do that. But neither could he ordain men priests, for the simple reason that the Jewish priests at that time were priests by descent. The priesthood was hereditary, in other words.

Kamada In any case, if he thought the world would come to an end in that generation...

Whitland Quite. And when, after his death, his followers found that, after all, the world was not coming to an end, they gradually established a new set of offices from which the hierarchy of overseers, elders and servants eventually emerged.

Hiraoka Overseers? Elders?

Whitland Well, we know them better by their Greek names: bishops, priests and deacons. But these words were not even in Jesus' vocabulary.

Hiraoka Were any of these offices held by women?

Whitland As far as I know, only one female deacon gets a brief mention in the New Testament, where Paul recommends her to 'all God's beloved people in Rome'. But there were certainly no women overseers or elders.

I have to emphasise, however, that this whole arrangement of overseers and elders came into being some years after Jesus' death. It could hardly have been explicitly formulated before the destruction of the

Temple in Jerusalem in 70 AD, even if it was foreshadowed before that event.

So I hope I am not claiming too much if I say that there is nothing in Jesus' teaching to indicate how any kind of human institution is to be organised after his death. He preached the arrival of a divine kingdom, not a mundane polity. He made no mention of priests in this kingdom, whether men or women, although he did imply that some of his followers would be servants there.

Hiraoka So the women who followed him in his lifetime had no special status, I suppose. But I find it remarkable that there is even any reference at all to these women, especially if they were on the margin of society.

Whitland Dr Carla Ricci has a convincing argument about why these women disciples are mentioned when they are mentioned, and why they are passed over in silence, as they usually are. She shows that there is a conspiracy of silence regarding them, not only in the Gospels themselves but in all the commentaries on the Gospels that have been published in the last 100 years or more.

Hiraoka I look forward to reading her book!

Whitland Other writers have pointed out that Jesus did not make any obvious distinction between men and women in his behaviour towards them. He certainly does not put forward any generalisations about them. In the Gospels, there is no doctrine about women, no policy statement!

But in another part of the New Testament, in a letter written by Saint Paul to one of the first Christian congregations at Corinth, in Greece, you find this, for instance:

> *I want you to know that the head of every man is Christ, the head of*
> *woman is the man, and the head of Christ is God.*

I cannot say that I understand this, but it does seem to be attempting some kind of statement about women in general, and to be making them subordinate to men in general.

Kamada Yes, that much does seem clear.

Whitland And you will not find the Jesus of the Gospels venturing into such male chauvinist territory. Neither can you enlist him in the twentieth-century feminist camp. What an American humorist has called 'the war between men and women' was no concern of his.

If I am right about this, I think it is in accord with one of the most distinctive features of Jesus' behaviour and teaching, as portrayed in the Gospels — his emphasis on the individual person and the specific deed. More or less facile generalisations about classes of human beings are not in his style.

Chapter 21

~

Mary Magdalene

Kamada At our last meeting, you said that according to Luke's Gospel, Jesus was accompanied on his travels by a number of women. Dr Hiraoka would like to know more about these women, if that is possible, given that there seems to be a conspiracy of silence about them.

Hiraoka Yes. For example, are they identified in any way?

Whitland Well, Luke names some of them: Mary Magdalene, for instance. But Luke also says there were many other women with Jesus.

Hiraoka Mary Mag... Excuse me, that is a difficult name for me.

Whitland We have met her before, if you remember. In the unofficial Gospel of Philip, she was said to have been the partner of Jesus.

Kamada Ah, yes. But in the Gospels that we are discussing?

Whitland Those Gospels do not really tell us a great deal about her, and their accounts of her differ in some important details. This is why Susan Haskins begins her 500-page book on the subject — a masterpiece of beguiling erudition, by the way — with the sentence: 'We know very little about Mary Magdalen.'

Yet after Mary the mother of Jesus, Mary Magdalene is the most famous woman in the Gospels. But it is in later Christian traditions that she has been blown up into an almost entirely mythical figure, 'a beautiful woman with long golden hair', Susan Haskins says, 'weeping for her sins, the very incarnation of the age-old equation between feminine beauty, sexuality and sin' or, as another learned writer, Marina Warner, so well puts it, 'the prototype of the penitent whore'.

Marina Warner goes on to refer to Mary Magdalene as featuring in a particular kind of writing about Christian saints that 'so neatly condenses Christianity's fear of women, its identification of physical beauty with temptation, and its practice of bodily mortification'.

Hiraoka But in the Gospels...?

Whitland In terms of the chronological sequence of Jesus' ministry, the first mention of Mary Magdalene occurs in the passage in Luke's Gospel that I have just mentioned. She is identified there by her place of birth, Magdala, a fishing village on the north-west shore of the lake of Galilee, and by the fact that 'seven demons — or evil spirits — had come out of her'.

But Mary Magdalene's Gospel fame does not depend on the seven demons. In Mark, Matthew and John she is listed among the women present at the crucifixion of Jesus.

It is in the events reported after Jesus' death, however, that she plays her most important role. As Susan Haskins puts it, she 'was a witness — indeed, according to the Gospel of St John, the witness — of his resurrection, and was the first to be charged with the supreme ministry, that of proclaiming the Christian message. She brought the knowledge that through Christ's victory over death, life everlasting was offered to all who believe.'

The four Gospels do not agree in every detail about what happened on the first day of the week after Jesus was crucified, and a great deal has been written about these discrepancies, but it is far beyond my scope to weigh one Gospel account of the central events of the Christian religion against another.

Kamada But I think you have not finished your account of Mary Magdalene.

Whitland Well now: Mark states expressly that Mary Magdalene and Mary the mother of Joseph were watching when Jesus' body was laid in a tomb cut out of rock, and he continues his account:

> *When the Sabbath was over, Mary Magdalene, Mary the mother of James, and Salome bought aromatic spices, so that they could go and anoint him. And very early on the first day of the week, they come to the tomb when the sun had risen. And they were saying to one another, 'Who will roll away the stone for us from the entrance to the tomb?' And looking up, they see that the stone has been rolled away, because it was very big. And on entering the tomb they saw a young man sitting on the right-hand side, wearing a white robe; and they were astounded. But he says to them, 'Don't be amazed. You are looking for Jesus of Nazareth, who was crucified. He has risen, he is not here. Look, [that is] the place where they put him. But go, tell his disciples and Peter: "He is going ahead of you to Galilee; you will see him there, as he told you."' And the women came out and fled from the tomb, because they were beside themselves with fear. And they said nothing to anybody, because they were afraid.*

The Gospel by the author traditionally known as Mark ends at this point, but some verses added by another writer, which are missing from some manuscripts, state that when Jesus had risen from the dead, he 'appeared first to Mary Magdalene, from whom he had thrown out seven demons. She went and told those who had been with him, who were mourning and weeping. And when they heard that he was alive and had been seen by her, they did not believe her.'

Kamada At some time, perhaps not today, I should like to hear more about the seven demons.

Hiraoka And about Sarome, please...

Whitland Sarome? Oh, Salome! I'm afraid this is the only mention of her by name in the Gospels — this mention in Mark. There is another Salome, of course — the dancing girl...

But as for Mary Magdalene, Matthew's and Luke's versions of events on the morning of the resurrection differ in some details from Mark's, and I shall not dwell on them. You see, it is in John's Gospel that Mary Magdalene plays a unique role.

At times his Gospel, which was almost certainly written some decades after the others, seems to be deliberately correcting them on points of detail. For example, he says it was still dark when Mary Magdalene came to the tomb, whereas Mark states quite clearly that the sun had risen, and Matthew says it was after the Sabbath, as day was breaking.

What is more important, in John's Gospel, only Mary Magdalene comes to the tomb, and at this point, no young man appears, or men in shining clothes, as Luke reports. And according to John, when Mary Magdalene saw that the stone had been moved away from the tomb, she went running to Peter and to 'the other disciple, the one Jesus loved' — traditionally believed to be John himself.

Peter and the other disciple then run to the tomb. The other disciple ran faster than Peter, we are told, and reached the tomb first. But Peter was the first to enter the tomb, and he saw the linen cloths in which Jesus' body had been bound lying on the floor. The other disciple then went into the tomb, and, says John, 'he saw, and he believed... . The disciples then went back home.'

The Gospel continues:

> *But Mary was standing outside the tomb, near it, and weeping. Then,*
> *as she wept, she stooped to look into the tomb, and sees two angels*
> *in white seated [there], one at the head and one at the feet, where the*
> *body of Jesus had been lying. And they say to her, 'Woman, why are*
> *you weeping?' She says to them, 'Because they have taken my Lord*
> *away, and I don't know where they have put him.' After saying this,*
> *she turned her back, and sees Jesus standing [there], and she did not*
> *know that it was Jesus. Jesus says to her: 'Woman, why are you*
> *weeping? Who are you looking for?' She, thinking he was the gardener,*
> *says to him, 'Sir, if it is you who carried him off, tell me where you*
> *have put him, and I will go and take him away.' Jesus says to her,*
> *'Mary!' She turned and says to him in Hebrew, 'Rabbouni!' which*
> *means 'Teacher!' Jesus says to her, 'Do not cling to me, because I have*
> *not gone up to the Father yet. But go to my brothers and tell them,*
> *I am going up to my Father and your Father and my God and your*
> *God.' Mary Magdalene comes to the disciples and tells them, 'I have*
> *seen the Lord' and that he said these things to her.*

This is the last mention of Mary Magdalene in the Gospels, but from the earliest days of Christian belief she began to exert a fascination on men's minds, and to be the source of more or less sensational legends going very far beyond the little that is said about her in the Gospels. These are fully described and documented in the book about her by Susan Haskins, who emphasises that, 'Every interpretation that has accumulated around her reflects only the imagination of subsequent writers and their own historical context.'

Hiraoka But although the Gospels say little about her, what they do say is important, is it not?

Whitland Yes, indeed. And both Carla Ricci and Susan Haskins rightly stress the fact that, 'Unlike the eleven male disciples who feared for their own lives, the women disciples followed, were present at the crucifixion, witnessed the burial, discovered the empty tomb and, as true disciples, were rewarded with the first news of the resurrection and, in the case of Mary Magdalene, their first meeting with the risen Christ.'

Hiraoka In the context of our discussions, these comments are very interesting.

Whitland And important, too, in the wider context of the origins of the Christian religion.

Chapter 22

Salome, the dancing princess

Kamada Dr Hiraoka presents her apologies, but she is indisposed today. Perhaps we could take this opportunity to discuss something less important...

Whitland My dear professor! I am not sure that anything in the Gospels comes into that category.

Kamada I meant, less important from the point of view of the research project that she's taking part in. I was thinking, for example, of the dancing girl you alluded to when we were talking about Mary Magdalene.

Whitland Yes, the other Salome. She was the girl who danced in front of her stepfather, the client King of Galilee, Herod Antipas, and pleased him and his dinner party guests so much that, according to Mark, he told her, 'Ask me for whatever you want, and I'll give it to you.' Herod capped his promise with an oath, and — so the story runs — said he would give Salome as much as half his kingdom, if she asked for it.

Kamada It seems an exaggerated reward for a dance, but perhaps Herod had had too much to drink!

Whitland Or perhaps Mark made this bit up, borrowing it from an

Old Testament story about a Persian king who made the same promise, in exactly the same words, to his Jewish wife, Esther.

Although the Gospels do not say so, Salome was only about fourteen or fifteen at the time of this story. She was of royal blood herself, but presumably not used to receiving extravagant promises, because she had to get her mother, Herodias, to tell her what to ask the king for.

Herodias had left her first husband (who was also her uncle) for Herod Antipas (who was her cousin, and divorced from his first wife), and Mark reports that her marriage to Herod Antipas was denounced by John the Baptist, the prophet who was the cousin and forerunner of Jesus.

For this reason, Herodias bore a heavy grudge against John, and wanted to kill him. He was already in prison at her instigation, but Herod was afraid to kill him, as he knew John was a holy man. More than that, Herod took pleasure in hearing John talk, although there was a lot of what John said that he did not understand.

Kamada The Gospel actually says that? It is a pleasing detail.

Whitland Mark says this, but Matthew imputes another motive to Herod — he says Herod was afraid of the mob. Anyway, when Salome sought her mother's advice, Herodias told her to ask for the head of John the Baptist.

Mark continues the story:

> The girl at once hurried back to the king and made her request with
> the words, 'I want you to give me John the Baptist's head
> immediately, on a plate.' The king was grief-stricken, but because of
> his oath and the guests at his table, he did not want to break his word.
> And immediately the king sent a soldier of the guard with orders to
> bring the head in. The solder went off and beheaded him in the prison,
> and brought his head on a plate, and gave it to the girl, and the girl
> gave it to her mother.

The echo of the Old Testament story in the book of Esther suggests an element of folklore, but taken purely in the Gospel setting, Salome's story succeeds in striking an individual note, in spite of the fact that both Matthew and Mark tell it in notably restrained language. Any erotic suggestions are left entirely to the reader's imagination: all that is said is that Salome 'pleased' Herod and his guests.

Kamada The best erotic writing always leaves more unsaid than said.

Whitland Yes, but I am not sure that the authors of the Gospels were aiming at this particular effect!

As you know, the story has given rise to countless legendary versions and to famous treatments in works of art such as Gustave Flaubert's story *Hérodias*, and Oscar Wilde's play *Salome*, which he wrote in French. It was translated into English by Wilde's lover Lord Alfred Douglas, and later formed the libretto of the opera by Richard Strauss.

Flaubert is said to have drawn inspiration from a sculpture of Salome dancing on her hands that adorned a recess above one of the side doors of the cathedral in his native city of Rouen. But Flaubert's actual description of Salome's quivering breasts and belly 'rippling like the swell of the sea' owes much to his encounter at Esneh in Egypt with a *petite princesse* who asked him if he would care for a little 'fantasia', and danced wantonly for him as the prelude to a night of love-making.

The Salome of the Gospels, who is known to history from other sources, is not named by either Mark or Matthew: she is referred to simply as the daughter of Herodias. Perhaps both these Gospel writers wanted to avoid any possible confusion in the reader's mind between this Salome and the Salome who was a follower of Jesus, was present at the crucifixion, and was among the women who visited Jesus' empty tomb at sunrise on the first day of the week.

Chapter 23

Chapter 23

Jesus and the street-walker

Whitland The story of Salome, the dancer, is one of the very few episodes in the Gospels where, to the modern mind at least, an erotic note is struck.

Kamada In view of the general attitude to sex that the Gospels display, it is surprising that there are any hints at all of the erotic impulse.

Whitland One episode that I have in mind is the story of the woman who gate-crashed the Pharisee's dinner party, where Jesus was a guest.

Kamada So! But please tell me first what is meant by a Pharisee.

Whitland The Pharisees were Jews of what might be called the lower middle-class, in modern terms — below the landowning class, but above the illiterate masses of farm labourers, hired hands and so on. They were particularly associated with the synagogues, the popular centres of Jewish prayer and religious instruction that flourished in towns and villages.

They believed in the immortality of the individual soul and in physical, bodily resurrection. The American historian Salo Wittmayer Baron goes as far as to call this 'the fundamental conception of Pharisaism', and he adds: 'The idea of judgement and retribution after death is also of crucial significance. It is pushed so far as to exclude the wicked from resurrection.'

But I believe I have already mentioned the Pharisees at one of our meetings — they were a group that Jesus, not at this dinner party but on another occasion, cursed seven times.

Kamada As their belief in the resurrection of the body is the very basis of the Christian religion, I would have expected the Gospels to present the Pharisees in a favourable light.

Whitland But after the destruction of the Temple by the Romans in the year 70, the Christian congregations were usually at odds with the synagogues, and it seems most likely that these controversies have been projected back by the Gospel writers into the lifetime of Jesus, with the result that on the whole the Pharisees get a bad press.

They come off worst in Matthew's Gospel, where at one point Jesus compares them, famously, with whitewashed tombs. The most frequent charge against them is that of hypocrisy, and although Luke sometimes presents the Pharisees in a more favourable light than Matthew, it is in his Gospel that Jesus tells the parable of the Pharisee and the tax collector. The Pharisee thanks God that he is not like the rest of the human race, who are grasping, unjust, and wife-swappers; whereas the tax collector begs God to have mercy on him, for the wrong he has done.

It is this parable, more than any other passage in the Gospels, that has given the word 'pharisaical' or its equivalent the meaning 'self-righteous hypocrite' in every European language.

Kamada Thank you. Now, you were going to tell me about a woman who invited herself to a dinner party...

Whitland Oh yes! Let me see... Yes, the woman in question is described quite simply by Luke, who is the only Gospel writer to report the incident, as a 'sinner' who was 'in town'. 'Sinner' is what the older translations into English also call her; but for some reason modern translators try to describe her more obliquely: 'a woman known in the town as a bad woman', or 'a woman who was living an immoral life in the town', or 'a woman who had a bad name in the town'.

One modern commentator, however, deduces from a careful reading of the whole passage that the woman was indeed a prostitute — perhaps we could call her a street-walker in view of the reference to the town. One indication is that she was apparently wearing her hair loose, 'a sign of her fallen status, as only prostitutes wore their hair thus in public'.

Uninvited, the woman entered the house where Jesus and the other guests were reclining to eat, as people did in the ancient world. She was carrying a jar of ointment, and went and stood behind Jesus. She began to weep and to wash Jesus' feet with her tears, and then wiped away the tears with her hair. Then she covered his feet with kisses and rubbed the ointment over them.

Kamada As you relate it, this is certainly a powerfully erotic scene.

Whitland This is not my description, but Luke's. I am translating his words literally, and in a form that I hope conveys the atmosphere of the original.

Luke goes on:

When the Pharisee who had invited Jesus saw this, he said to himself, 'If this guy was a prophet, he'd know who this woman is who is mauling him, and what kind of woman she is — because she's a prostitute.'

But Jesus answered him: 'Simon, I've got something to say to you. There were two men in debt to a moneylender. One owed him 500 dollars, and the other, 50. As neither of them had any money to pay him back, he let them both off. So which of the two will love him more?' Simon answered, 'I suppose the one who was let off more.' Jesus said, 'Correct!'

Then he turned to the woman and said to Simon, 'You see this woman? I came into your house; you didn't give me any water for my feet; but she washed my feet with her tears and wiped them dry with her hair. You did not give me a kiss; but she has not stopped covering my feet with kisses since the moment she came in. You did not rub my head with oil; but she has rubbed my feet with ointment. For this reason, I tell you, her many sins are forgiven, because she loved a lot. The person who is forgiven little, shows little love.'

Then Jesus said to the woman, 'Your sins are forgiven.' The other dinner guests began to say to themselves, 'Who is this man, who even forgives sins?' But Jesus said to the woman, 'Your faith has saved you: go in peace.'

One strange thing about this story, as Luke tells it, is that the parable of the debtors makes the point that greater forgiveness earns greater love, while the point of the prostitute's story is that greater love earns greater forgiveness. It looks as if two separate stories — the parable and the prostitute's arrival at the dinner party — have somehow got muddled by Luke.

Kamada Yet this does not diminish the effectiveness of the story.

Whitland The love the woman showed for Jesus is, of course, *agape* — the non-sexual love, the only love admitted by the Gospel writers. Yet the language in which this episode is conveyed is unusually sensual — perhaps uniquely for the Gospels.

There is one particular difficulty, however, in trying to convey the flavour of the original Greek. A modern writer, attempting to describe an episode of this kind, would be almost certain to resort to some colourful adjectives and adverbs. But in the Greek here, the impact is achieved only by verbs and nouns. There is not one single descriptive adjective or adverb in the whole passage.

Because it is irrelevant to his purpose in recounting the incident, the Gospel writer does not say whether Jesus himself was aroused sexually, as most men would be, by the woman's behaviour.

Some time after the Gospels were written, the idea arose that the unnamed prostitute was Mary Magdalene. Some incidental details in the Gospel encouraged this view without actually authenticating it; but once the idea had taken hold it blossomed into an elaborate tradition which has been explored in impressive detail by Susan Haskins in her book *Mary Magdalen.*

Chapter 24

☞

Jesus and prostitutes

Whitland Ben Witherington the Third, the immensely learned author of *Women in the Ministry of Jesus*, has expressed the hope that through investigating the attitude of Jesus towards women as reflected in his teaching, 'we should be able to begin to evaluate the way Jesus thought the new demands of the Kingdom would affect women in their roles as mothers, daughters, wives, widows, harlots and believers' — and he apparently sees nothing strange in this limited and prejudicial list of women's roles.

Kamada If this list is prejudicial to women, it is just as well that Dr Hiraoka is not with us again today. You have gathered, perhaps, that she is a feminist, in spite of her demure manner. But I am not sure that I have understood you completely. Did you say 'harlots'?

Whitland It is an old-fashioned word for prostitute. There is nothing in the Gospels to suggest that Jesus was afraid to use the word 'prostitute' — on the contrary. But the committee that produced the *New English Bible* evidently was: where the word occurs in the plural in Luke, they translate it 'women'. But perhaps these translators, who are not named in my edition, thought that the two words 'prostitute' and 'woman' were interchangeable in some contexts.

Kamada Surely not! This would be an extreme example of the low view of women that some Christian apologists seem to take!

Whitland Here is a curious detail, but one which seems to have attracted very little comment: in opening his Gospel, Matthew traces Jesus' lineage back through his father Joseph to Abraham, and Joseph even counts a prostitute — Rahab — in his remote ancestry. I say, 'Jesus' father', but according to Christian belief, of course, he was Jesus' father only in a legal sense — not in a natural sense.

Kamada All the same, it is interesting that there is a prostitute in Jesus' legal lineage, if I can use such an expression. In some religions, there are sacred prostitutes, associated with places of worship. Was Rahab one of these?

Whitland No. Rahab was a Canaanite — a member of one of the tribes who lived in the country that, according to Israelite belief, had been promised to them by God. Sacred prostitution was known in Canaan at that time, but there is nothing in the biblical account of Rahab to suggest that she was associated in her trade with any cult. For one thing, she did not live in a temple. But in any case, she is described as a common prostitute, not as a sacred temple prostitute — these are two separate words in Hebrew.

Her story is told in one of the early books of the Old Testament. She had a house built into the city wall of Jericho, and when two Israelite spies came to check the place out, she hid them from the king of Jericho under some flax on the roof of her house — it's difficult to picture the roof of a house built into a city wall, but there it is. Rahab's reason for doing this was that she had heard all about the Israelites' god, Yahweh, and she was sure that her own people, the Canaanites and, it must be supposed, their gods, were no match for him.

Rahab became a folk heroine among the Jews: Paul says that it was her faith that made her receive the spies in peace, and another New

Testament writer says she was justified by her deeds. Both these writers refer to Rahab as 'Rahab the prostitute'. But the Jews were expressly forbidden to allow the practice of sacred prostitution, whether by women or by men, and I don't think Paul would have written about Rahab in the way he did, if she had been a temple prostitute.

Kamada You seemed to imply just now that Jesus, too, used the word 'prostitute'.

Whitland Yes, I was referring to his famous parable of the prodigal son. Beautiful though this parable is, it is recorded only by Luke. Luke makes Jesus paint a vivid scene of the errant son's final return home after a life of debauchery in a distant foreign country, where his extravagance had reduced him to starvation. His father gives him a tremendous welcome, and this incenses his older brother, who had stayed at home to look after the farm.

This older son complains bitterly to his father: 'You haven't given me so much as a young goat, to have a barbecue with my pals. But when this son of yours turns up, after getting through his share of your fortune with prostitutes, for him you slaughter the calf we've been specially fattening up.'

To this, the young men's father makes his famous reply: 'You're with me the whole time. But we had to celebrate, because your brother was dead, and is now alive; and he was lost, but has been found.'

Kamada There must be a reason why the other Gospel writers fail to record this powerful parable.

Whitland Perhaps. But Luke has several long parables that the other Gospels do not recount.

But not only does Jesus use the word 'prostitutes' in this parable recorded by Luke, but elsewhere in the Gospels he refers sympathetically to them. I should explain that two kinds of people are singled out in the Gospels as 'sinners', that is to say habitually wicked or godless: tax collectors and prostitutes.

Apart from the subscriptions made by Jews throughout the world to the funds of the Temple at Jerusalem, the Roman authorities levied various taxes. In Galilee, where Jesus spent most of his ministry, the taxes that hit people the hardest were tolls or duties charged on goods moved into and out of the province. So one should think of the tax collectors of the Gospels as more like customs and excise men — even VAT inspectors in the United Kingdom — than income tax collectors in today's world.

In his book *The Historical Figure of Jesus*, Professor Sanders argues convincingly that these customs officers were held in such low regard in Jesus' time because they were 'routinely dishonest'.

Kamada It is highly probable.

Whitland The expression 'tax collectors and sinners' often crops up in the Gospels, in a way that suggests that readers at the time knew who these other 'sinners' were. Jesus himself was accused by some of the stricter Jews of eating and drinking with tax collectors and sinners. In Matthew's Gospel, Jesus refers to himself as one who came eating and drinking, and then adds that people say of him, 'Look, a glutton and a wine drinker, a friend of tax collectors and sinners.'

Who were these sinners? Perhaps they were people who simply did not come up to the strict standards of the ultra-pious Pharisees — the powerful religious group that we have already encountered, who are portrayed in the Gospels as Jesus' main opponents. But the only category of persons that the Gospels single out as generally wicked was prostitutes. It is nowhere explicitly stated that Jesus associated regularly with prostitutes, but it is possible that some of these sinners he was accused of befriending were prostitutes.

In one particularly striking passage in Matthew, Jesus tells the Jewish chief priests and senior citizens: 'Tax collectors and prostitutes go into the Kingdom of God ahead of you.' He tells them why: it is because the tax collectors and prostitutes believed Jesus' cousin and forerunner, the desert preacher John, who proclaimed the ritual of baptism as a sign of turning away from wrongdoing, whereas the chief priests did not.

Kamada I find it strange that tax collectors and prostitutes are mentioned together — what was the link between them?

Whitland One explanation that occurs to me is this: in some parts of the ancient world there was a special tax on prostitutes, or on brothel keepers. If there was such a tax in Galilee, or even a more general tax to which prostitutes were liable, some of the tax collectors may have accepted sexual favours from prostitutes instead of tax payments.

It may be objected that there is no mention of a brothel tax in Palestine in our ancient sources, but the whole subject of taxation there is very poorly documented. There was apparently such a tax in Athens in the fourth century before our era, but we would not know about it but for a passing mention by a public speaker.

The Gospels are not the only ancient books to link tax collectors with prostitutes: the second-century satirist Lucian writing in Greek also couples them with 'adulterers and pimps, flatterers and toadies'.

Chapter 25

☙

The woman with expensive perfume

Kamada Dr Hiraoka has been reading the notes I made on our last two conversations, and has shown me another story, not in Luke this time, but in the other Gospels. It is remarkably similar in some of its detail to Luke's story.

Hiraoka Yes. This story also relates to a dinner party, and it is strange that the host has the same name, Simon, in both cases. But in Luke's Gospel, this Simon is introduced as a Pharisee, whereas in Mark and Matthew, he is called a leper. They are not the same thing, are they — Pharisee and leper?

Whitland Hardly! Most modern commentators take 'leper' to mean not necessarily more than 'suffering from a skin disease'. Perhaps many people in Palestine in those days were afflicted in that way and some of them were, no doubt, Pharisees, but...

I think a likelier explanation of the parallels between the two different dinner party stories is that both these incidents derive ultimately from the same happening, but the story gave rise to different versions as it was passed round by word of mouth. The confused moral that Luke draws from his story already points to some crossed lines, but they can no longer be unravelled.

But please give me a moment to look at the story as Mark tells it, because I assume that Matthew and perhaps John drew on his version when they were writing their own Gospels.

Hiraoka Here is the chapter in Mark.

Whitland Thank you. Now let me find it in the Greek text... Yes, here it is:

While Jesus was reclining at table in Bethany, in the house of Simon the leper, a woman came in with a bottle of expensive ointment — oil of spikenard. She broke the bottle open and poured the oil over his head. Some people there were annoyed, and said to one another, 'What was the point of wasting the ointment like that? This ointment could have been sold for more than 300 dollars, and the money could have been given to the poor.' And they growled indignantly at her. But Jesus said, 'Leave her alone. Why do you create difficulties for her? She has done something beautiful to me. You have the poor with you always, and you can do them good whenever you like, but you will not always have me. She has done what she had in her power to do. She has prepared my body for burial in advance. In fact I tell you that wherever the gospel is proclaimed to the whole world, what she did will also be told as a memorial to her.'

Does the last sentence, I wonder, report a genuine saying of Jesus? In only one other place does he refer to his teaching as 'the gospel'.

Kamada But a greater problem for me is that Jesus expected the world to end within a generation. So who is going to tell the woman's story? And the woman remains anonymous — so what is the use of her memorial?

Whitland And the plot thickens when we turn to John's version. Here it is, in the twelfth chapter. The incident is still placed in Bethany, but Jesus' hosts are now Mary and Martha, the sisters of Lazarus, who had been brought back to life by Jesus on the fourth day after his death.

It is Mary who brings in the ointment, and she pours it not over his head, as in Mark, but over his feet, like the prostitute in Luke's story. Like the prostitute, too, she also wipes Jesus' feet with her hair — the wording here is exactly the same as Luke's, with a verb which means 'to wipe off, to wipe away', or 'to wipe dry'.

In Mark's version, the guests who objected are not named, although some Gospel manuscripts identify them as Jesus' disciples. But in John, the objection is raised by Judas Iscariot, the disciple who was fated, the Gospels say, to betray Jesus. John attributes a sinister motive to Judas: he did not care about the poor, but as he was in charge of the disciples' money-box, he would have stolen some of the money that would have been raised.

In John's account of the incident, too, Jesus tells Judas to let Mary alone, so that she 'may keep the ointment for the day of my burial'. This has been interpreted as 'establishing Mary of Bethany's prophetic and prescient role: in anointing him in his lifetime, she witnesses her knowledge of his death and resurrection'.

Kamada The various versions of this story must provide some interesting clues as to how the Gospels were put together.

Whitland Yes, there can be no doubt that the differences in detail between these versions reflect their authors' hidden agenda. Luke has used the underlying story to add detail to his picture of the Pharisees — a rather complex picture, as it happens. John has used it to present Judas Iscariot as a man who had been odious even before his thoughts turned to betraying Jesus — he calls him quite bluntly 'a thief'.

I am afraid that this is in keeping with a general trend in John's Gospel to blacken the Jews. As a modern writer has put it, 'The expansion of Judas' money-corruption was a most fateful development for the history of anti-Semitism.'

165

Chapter 26

Mary and Martha

Kamada You referred yesterday to the sisters of the man Lazarus, and you said that Jesus brought this man back to life a few days after he had died. Dr Hiraoka would like to know more about these women and to learn how they reacted to this astounding miracle. Is anything more said about these sisters in the Gospels?

Whitland Yes. As far as I can tell, Mary and Martha, as they are named, are the only women in the Gospels that Jesus is said, in so many words, to have loved. This is what John says, and some commentators have found it especially significant. But he is not, of course, implying anything sexual.

Hiraoka But it is an interesting statement, all the same. And you said that one of the sisters poured ointment over Jesus' feet and then wiped them dry with her hair?

Whitland Yes. That is also reported by John, in the chapter after the one about Lazarus. But in the Lazarus chapter, after saying that Mary and Martha lived in the village of Bethany, and that Lazarus had fallen ill, John says his sisters sent a message to Jesus: 'Look, Lord, the man you love is ill.'

John continues:

When Jesus heard, he said, 'This illness is not going to make him die, but it is for the glory of God, so that the son of God may be glorified by means of it.'

Kamada When he says 'the son of God', he is referring to himself?

Whitland Yes. And John goes on:

Jesus loved Martha and her sister and Lazarus. So when he heard that he was ill, then he stayed where he was for two days. After this, he says to his disciples, 'Let's go back to Judaea.' The disciples say to him, 'Rabbi, just now the Jews were trying to stone you, and you're going back there again?'

Jesus says to them, 'Our friend Lazarus has fallen asleep, but I am going to wake him.' So his disciples said to him, 'Lord, if he has fallen asleep, he will be all right.' But Jesus had been talking about the death of Lazarus, but they thought he was talking about sleep in the literal sense. So then Jesus told them plainly, 'Lazarus has died. And for your sake I'm glad that I wasn't there — so that you may believe. But let's go to him.'

Kamada These remarks about sleep and death do sound as if they are part of a well preserved tradition.

Whitland The mixture of tenses, too — Jesus says... Jesus told them — is, I think, a traditional mode of narrative. And it's interesting that, as the story unfolds, John claims to report the actual wording of exchanges between Jesus and one of the sisters:

When Jesus arrived, he found that Lazarus had already been in the tomb for four days. Bethany was near Jerusalem — about a mile and three-quarters away — and a lot of Jews had come to visit Martha and Mary to console them about their brother. So when Martha heard that Jesus was coming, she went to meet him. But Mary stayed at home.

So Martha said to Jesus, 'Lord, if you had been here, my brother would not have died. And even now I know that whatever you ask God for, God will give you.' Jesus says to her, 'Your brother will rise again.' Martha says to him, 'I know he will rise again at the rising from the dead on the last day.'

Jesus said to her, 'I am the rising from the dead and the life. He that believes in me, even if he dies, will live; and every person living and believing in me will not die in eternity. Do you believe this?'

She says to him, 'Yes, Lord. I believe you are the Messiah, the son of God, who has come into the world.'

Kamada If you will allow me to say so, this narrative is turning Martha into a theologian. Because she not only accepts Jesus' claim to be the conqueror of death, but she implies that he is a being from another world. But is that a possible belief for a Jewess in first-century Palestine?

Whitland Well, all sorts of ideas about the Messiah were current at that time. You are thinking perhaps of the manifestation of a divine being that there is in Hinduism — the *avatar* who quite literally descends from the world above. It is possible, I suppose, that some Jews thought in similar terms, but impossible to say how clear or how wide-spread such a notion would have been.

But you have a point when you say that Martha is making a theo-logical statement.

Kamada Is Martha making it, or John, the author of this Gospel?

Whitland It's true that John makes Jesus speak more than once of 'the Father who has sent me', and the implication of much of what he says is that he has come from another world.

And as John's narrative continues, Martha again speaks in what is an echo of theological language:

> *Martha called Mary, her sister, and told her in secrecy, 'The teacher is here and is asking for you.'*

The word Martha uses here foreshadows the later theological term *parousia* — the presence, and later, the second coming of the Messiah. But now, John's narrative turns to Martha's sister Mary. She also goes out of the village to meet Jesus, and repeats Martha's remark that Lazarus would not have died if Jesus had been there.

John continues:

> *So when Jesus saw her weeping, and the Jews who had come with her weeping, he was deeply moved in his spirit, and he was troubled, and said, 'Where have you put him?' They say to him, 'Lord, come and see.' Jesus shed tears. So the Jews said, 'See how he loved him!' And some of them said, 'Couldn't he, who opened the eyes of the blind man, have done something to prevent Lazarus' death?'*

Hiraoka Here is one of the rare descriptions of Jesus' inner feelings.

Whitland Yes. This is the only time that we're told that Jesus wept. And John dwells on Jesus' sorrow:

> *So Jesus, deeply moved again, comes to the tomb. It was a cave, and a stone was lying against it. The sister of the dead man, Martha, says to him, 'Lord, he's already stinking! He's been dead four days.' Jesus says to her, 'Didn't I tell you that if you believe, you will see the glory of God?' So they removed the stone.*

Then Jesus raised his eyes, and said, 'Father, I thank you for hearing me. I myself knew that you always hear me, but I spoke for the sake of the crowd standing round, for them to believe that you sent me.'

And having said this, he shouted at the top of his voice, 'Lazarus, here, come out!' The dead man came out, his hands and feet bound in bandages, and a towel round his face. Jesus says to them, 'Unbind him, and let him go.'

We are not told how Lazarus behaved on being brought back from the dead, but John reports that the raising of Lazarus from the dead made the official leaders of the Jews and some Pharisees meet and decide that Jesus would provoke the Roman authorities to destroy the Jewish nation, and that for that reason he must be put to death.

John also says that the chief priests of the Jews planned to put Lazarus to death, because the story of his return from the tomb was winning followers for Jesus.

Kamada In telling us about Lazarus, you have referred only to John's Gospel. Do the other Gospels add anything to his account? Or leave out anything important?

Whitland They say nothing at all about this Lazarus. The poor man Lazarus in the parable about the rich man in hell in Luke's Gospel is another person.

Kamada It is remarkable, then, that so impressive and decisive a miracle as the raising of Lazarus from the dead is reported only by John — there is no reference at all to it in the narrative Gospels?

Whitland Not the slightest. And after John's statement that the chief priests were planing to kill Lazarus, he allows him to disappear from his narrative. Lazarus makes no further appearances in the New

171

Testament, and nothing is told, for example, about his second death.

Some learned commentators have found it strange that there is no further mention of Lazarus and his family in the history of the early Christian Church, although there were later legends that he sailed for Cyprus with his sisters in a leaking boat, miraculously reached the island, and became bishop of Kitium. According to another legend, he became bishop of Marseilles.

Kamada His second experience of dying must have been exceptionally hard to endure, whether or not he was a bishop.

Whitland No doubt. But before we leave Lazarus, I should not forget to mention that Mary and Martha do make a brief but famous appearance in Luke's Gospel. This is the incident that has made Martha the proverbially fretful, overzealous housewife. Ah, I see that Dr Hiraoka is making notes!

Hiraoka Yes. But please do not let me interrupt you.

Whitland Well then... As Jesus and his disciples went along — Luke introduces the incident without giving it a specific time or place — he came to a certain village, and a certain woman, Martha by name, welcomed him into her house. She had a sister called Mary, who sat down at the Lord's feet and listened to him speaking.

But Martha was distracted with a lot of household tasks. And she stood near Jesus, and said, 'Lord, doesn't it bother you that my sister has left me to do all the serving by myself? So tell her to help me!' But in reply the Lord said, 'Martha, Martha, you are anxious and make a song and a dance about a lot of things, but one thing is needed. Because Mary has chosen the good part, which will not be taken away from her.'

Hiraoka And what is this one thing, this good part?

Whitland Evidently, to listen to Jesus, and to accept his teaching. In John's Gospel, Martha is presented as his disciple, but here in Luke, her sister Mary has that role. The repetition of Martha's name is interesting, but one cannot be certain about the tone of Jesus' voice. One modern translator gives 'Martha, my dear' as a translation of the repeated name in the original, but 'my dear' itself is open to more than one interpretation.

Martha, by the way, is the only woman in the Gospels to be addressed by name by Jesus, apart from Mary Magdalene after his resurrection.

Chapter 27

☞

The woman at the well

Kamada On Tuesday, you recounted the exchange of words between Jesus and the two sisters, Martha and Mary. Both Dr Hiraoka and I should like to know whether there are other episodes in the Gospels, where Jesus is heard in conversation with women?

Whitland In conversation? Let me think... Yes — there is one quite long conversation with a woman. Perhaps it is Jesus' longest actual exchange of words with anyone, male or female. And it is with a stranger Jesus meets at a well.

Hiraoka A stranger?

Whitland Yes. It's essential to the story that Jesus had never met this woman before. And she is not merely a stranger — she is a Samaritan: that is to say a foreigner from a country whose population, though of mixed origins, like most populations, was mainly descended from the ancient Israelites, but had severed its allegiance to Judaism. So the Samaritans were not only foreigners in the eyes of the Jews, but were looked on by them with the powerful mixture of hatred and contempt that is so often reserved for former brethren who have defected to form a sect of their own.

Kamada This happens in politics, too, or in any situation where there is meant to be some ideology subscribed to in common.

Whitland There is another point here. You see, to readers of this Gospel at the time that it was published, the fact that this stranger was a woman would have been as shocking — probably even more shocking than the fact that she was a Samaritan. That is why the Gospel writer, who is John, says that the disciples were amazed to find Jesus talking with a woman.

According to one modern commentator, 'it was considered highly undesirable' for a religious teacher to hold a conversation with a woman. The site of this encounter is also significant: a well was, and still is in some Mediterranean villages, the only place where an unaccompanied woman could be seen in public.

Kamada So the well is a realistic detail in the story.

Whitland Yes, but its primary purpose is symbolic. The well is not any old well. And I certainly do not need to enlarge on the symbolism of water.

As John tells the story, in his travels between Judaea and Galilee, Jesus comes to the town of Sychar in Samaria. There, at a well traditionally associated with Jacob, the father of the original twelve tribal chiefs of Israel, Jesus 'weary from walking' sat down to rest.

John continues:

It was about noon. A Samaritan woman came to draw water. Jesus says to her, 'Give me a drink.' His disciples had gone into the town to buy food. So the Samaritan woman said to him, 'How come that you, a Jew, ask me, a Samaritan woman, for a drink? Because Jews do not associate with Samaritans.' Jesus answered her: 'If you knew God's gift, and who is telling you to give him a drink, it is you who would have asked him, and he would have given you living water.'

176

Kamada 'Living water' — that is a beautiful expression.

Whitland Yes. And the woman is struck by these words, as John recounts:

> *The woman says to him: 'Sir, you have no bucket for drawing water, and the well is deep. So where do you get this living water? Perhaps you are greater than our ancestor Jacob, who gave us the well, and drank from it himself, and so did his sons and his sheep and goats?'*

> *Jesus answered her: 'Everyone who drinks from this water will be thirsty again; but whoever drinks from the water that I shall give him, will never be thirsty again; but the water that I shall give him will become in him a spring of water leaping to eternal life.'*

> *The woman says to him, 'Sir, give me this water, so that I may not be thirsty, or ever come here again to draw water.'*

Kamada The woman is evidently taking Jesus literally, at a rather practical level.

Hiraoka Yes. She would like not to have to fetch water in future!

Whitland Yes, and taken at its face value, the narrative descends at this point from its sublime level to something that, on a literal reading, is more like village gossip. Because Jesus now tells the woman to go and call her husband, and then come back to the well. The woman answers him:

> *'I haven't got a husband.' Jesus says to her, 'You were right to say you have no husband. Because you have had five husbands and the man you have now is not your husband. What you said was true.'*

> *The woman says to him, 'Sir, I see you are a prophet. Our ancestors*

177

worshipped on this mountain. And you Jews say that the place where one must worship is in Jerusalem.'

Hiraoka What does the woman mean by calling Jesus a prophet?

Whitland The experts — the theologians who have made a special study of John's Gospel — are divided on this point. John Marsh, for one, reads a tremendous amount into the woman's remark. He supposes that Jesus' reference to the woman's husband is a coded reference to the god of the Samaritans, that the woman is made aware of what he calls 'the ultimate poverty of her Samaritan religion', and that she comes to realise that 'she can no longer continue the pretence that the conversation is purely personal, and she proceeds to do what it is necessary to do in order to have the depth of the "Samaritan-Jewish" question exposed at its Christian depth.'

Hiraoka [*Whispers*]: *Chotto, matte kudasai!*

Kamada But can one speak of 'Christian depth' at a time when the word 'Christian' surely belonged to the future?

Whitland The whole of Marsh's commentary is a striking example of the theologian's urge towards maximum content that I believe I have already mentioned. It is symptomatic, too, that it leads him to say something that hardly makes sense in English.

But Marsh also reads a symbolic significance into the number five: according to him, the woman's five husbands represent the five foreign gods the king of Assyria imported into Samaria when he invaded it in the year 721 BC Another theologian has a problem with this, however. He counts seven gods, not five, in the Old Testament book that conveys this particular piece of information, and he points out that they arrived simultaneously in Samaria, whereas the woman's five husbands presumably turned up on the scene in succession.

It's true that Marsh quotes the Jewish historian Josephus in support of his contention that there were five gods, but Jesus could not have had Josephus in mind, as he was born a few years after Jesus' death. This leaves the rather remote possibility that Jesus was drawing on a tradition known also to Josephus, which was at variance with the Old Testament, but which he — Jesus — thought overruled the Old Testament account.

Kamada But in any case, the woman seems to talk not of different gods, but of different places of worship.

Whitland This was the most obvious religious difference between the Jews and the Samaritans. The Samaritans erected a temple of their own on Mount Gezirim, and this led to bitter religious rivalry between Jerusalem, where the Jews had their temple, and Gezirim.

But Jesus repudiates both these mountain-based cults, in a declaration that became fundamental to Christian belief. As John reports him, Jesus tells the Samaritan woman:

> *Believe me, woman, the hour is coming when you will worship the Father neither on this mountain nor in Jerusalem. You Samaritans worship what you do not know; we Jews worship what we do know. Because salvation comes from the Jews. But the hour is coming — and is already here — when true worshippers will worship the Father in spirit and in truth, because the Father seeks such worshippers. God is spirit, and those who worship him must worship in spirit and in truth.'*

Kamada Yes. It is an important text. But please go on reading.

Whitland The woman says to him, 'I know that the Messiah — the one called anointed — is coming. When he comes, he will tell us everything.' Jesus says to her: 'I who am talking to you am the Messiah.'

You know, this is the first time in John's Gospel that Jesus himself explicitly claims to be the Messiah.

Hiraoka And he makes this claim to a woman!

Kamada And to a foreigner.

Hiraoka But is that where the story ends?

Whitland No. At this point, Jesus' male disciples appear, and, as I said, were amazed that he was having a conversation with a woman. But, says John,

> *No one said, 'What are you after?' or 'What are you talking about with her?' So the woman left her water jar there and went away to the town, and tells the people, 'Come with me and see a man who told me everything I've ever done. Could he be the Messiah?' They left the town and came to see Jesus.*

Kamada These people were easily impressed. There could be several explanations of Jesus' clairvoyance... And I would not expect a deity descended from another world to resort to such tricks to establish his credentials.

Whitland But perhaps John has forestalled that objection, because he concludes his account of the incident in this way:

> *And from that town many of the Samaritans believed in him because of the woman's word, when she solemnly declared that he told her*

everything she had ever done. So when the Samaritans came to Jesus they asked him to stay with them, and he stayed for two days, and the majority believed because of his speech, and they told the woman that they no longer believed because of what she said, 'but because we have heard for ourselves, and we know that this man truly is the saviour of the world.'

Kamada I am still left wondering how this story entered the tradition. Jesus was alone with the woman during their conversation. So did he report it in detail to his disciples? And did John, the author of this Gospel, regard Jesus' clairvoyant insight into the woman's marital history as supernatural? Or did John invent the whole symbolic story for his own theological purposes? And I should also like to ask you to say more about the statement that salvation comes from the Jews.

Whitland Ah! Now that is a whole topic in itself!

Chapter 28

Was Jesus a racist?

Kamada After our last conversation, I knew there was an important point I hoped you would explain to us. According to Dr Hiraoka's notes, Jesus told the Samaritan woman, 'salvation comes from the Jews'. From a Japanese point of view, this is necessarily an exclusive doctrine.

Jesus taught that a new spiritual kingdom would be established, and Christians believe that they are to be the courtiers surrounding his throne, while millions of their fellow humans have never been presented and never will be presented at this court. Is this what Jesus believed?

Whitland No one will ever know whether Jesus actually made this remark, or whether it has been put into his mouth by John. But it has to be said that in the Gospels in general, Jesus is sometimes presented as accepting the common Jewish belief that they were the people singled out by Almighty God to establish his reign of justice.

On the other hand, however, Jesus certainly challenged conventional Jewish modes of thought when he made a non-Jew, a Samaritan, the exemplary hero of his most famous parable.

I say 'a non-Jew', but that is to understate the fact that in Jewish eyes the Samaritans were not just any non-Jews, but hateful sectarians. The goodness of the Samaritan in the parable is contrasted, moreover, with the behaviour of two Jewish priests who had failed to go to the help of a fellow Jew, left for dead by some muggers on the road from Jerusalem to Jericho.

There are, too, other sayings or deeds of Jesus that argue against attributing to him a narrowly tribal or racist attitude.

Kamada This is surely a topic that has to be considered in its historical context.

Whitland Yes. And perhaps I may say at the outset that in the ancient world, as in today's world, there were plenty of people who thought of themselves — their own nation or tribe — as superior to the rest of mankind and, in many cases, as having a divine right to lord it over them.

The successive empires of the area we now call the Middle East — Babylonian, Phoenician, Egyptian, Persian, Athenian, Alexandrian, Roman — were all to some extent motivated and sustained, so long as they were sustained, by ideas of this sort, culminating in the Roman belief that it was Rome's destiny 'to conquer the proud', by which they meant anyone who failed to recognise them as top dogs.

Kamada Well, I have to admit that we Japanese have also believed we have a special mission in the world, that our national spirit is unique...

Whitland But the ancient Jews gave notions of this sort a special character. They claimed to be specially chosen by the one and only God of heaven and earth to establish his all-embracing reign of justice — though there was more than one view as to how and when this state of affairs would be brought about.

At the time of Jesus, the hopes of the Jewish people, subject as they were to Roman rule, were for the most part centred on an 'anointed one' — the Messiah — who would be God's agent in delivering his people from servitude and restoring them to an upright and indeed holy life in his kingdom. But whether this Messiah would be 'a warrior hero, who would destroy his enemies and restore Israel's sovereignty over the world', or a supernatural being with the kind of fantastic cosmic credentials at that time attributed to Babylonian and Persian mythological figures, was the subject of a great deal of conflicting speculation between various groups of Jews.

It would be wrong, however, to read typically imperial territorial aspirations or claims into these Messianic hopes. It can be seen from Matthew's Gospel that it was possible for the Jews in Jesus' time to entertain a fanciful notion of 'all the kingdoms of the world and their glory'. But these kingdoms were not, when all is said and done, to be governed by an earthly king. God himself would be the emperor, if one thought in terms of empire — the reverse of the Roman practice that made the emperor a god.

Kamada The traditional view of the Emperor of Japan is that he is of divine descent.

Whitland Ideas of this kind obviously lend themselves to the promotion of one form or other of racism. And no doubt there was a racist element in these ancient Jewish beliefs, and in the Gospels the word 'race' does occur, when Mark calls the woman of Tyre whose daughter Jesus cured of a mental illness 'a Greek, a Syrophoenician by race'.

But the differences between human beings that the ancient Jews and other ancient peoples regarded as giving rise to differences of military, political, spiritual or intellectual worth were not linked to any scientific or would-be scientific notions of race, of course.

Kamada Well, it goes without saying that they did not have the faintest notion of chromosomes or genomes, or anything of that kind!

Whitland No, it would be truer to say of the ancients that it was the

185

other way round with them, when it came to explaining cause and effect in this sphere. For them, the military, social, spiritual, or intellectual worth of human beings did not so much depend on race as give rise to it — or give rise, at least, to the tribal or social bonds that were for them the reality.

In any case, whatever notions the ancient Jews, or any other ancient people for that matter, may have had about race, they were a long way from any present-day ideas on the subject, and it would be wrong to think of them as 'racists' in any modern sense.

Kamada But for all that, if I understand you, you are saying that the Jesus of the Gospels recognises the fact, if not of racial, I mean genetic differences, at least of tribal differences, which he is sometimes shown as acknowledging, and sometimes as denying. Is that right?

Whitland Yes, he recognises them, for example, in Matthew's Gospel, where he is said to have regarded himself as 'sent only to the lost sheep of the House of Israel' — a remark he made when refusing, at first, to cure the daughter of the Syrophoenician woman because she was not a Jewess. The same exclusion of non-Jews is to be found in the same Gospel when Jesus instructs his disciples to proclaim that the kingdom of the heavens is imminent:

> *Do not head for any Gentiles, and do not go into any Samaritan town.*
> *But go rather to the lost sheep of the House of Israel.*

There is also a curiously snide reference to the 'Gentiles of the world' when Jesus urges his followers to trust in providence, and not worry about what they will be able to eat or drink, or wear in the future — it is the Gentiles, he says, who wish for all these things.

By 'Gentiles' Jesus meant non-Jews. It is hardly a word still current in everyday English, but it is used in some modern English translations of the Gospels. Historically, the word 'Gentile' came into English when the first translators of the Bible, in the fourteenth century, found the word, or a related word, in the Latin version of it.

Kamada You mean that they translated from the Latin? Not from the Greek?

Whitland Yes. They used the fourth-century version of the Bible known as 'the published edition', which was a translation of the Hebrew Old Testament and the Greek New Testament into Latin made in the fifth century by Saint Jerome — though he also revised some earlier attempts.

Kamada But should we not go back to the Greek, to see what Jesus was saying here about non-Jews?

Whitland In the Gospel, the Greek word translated as 'Gentiles' is *ethne*, from which, of course, our English word 'ethnic' is derived. And this word in turn was used to translate the Hebrew word *goyim* when the Old Testament was translated into Greek, by the 72 Egyptian Jews who, according to the legend, carried out this task in 72 days.

In the Old Testament, non-Jews are often referred to as *goyim*. For example, when the author of the Psalms asks, 'Why do the nations rage?' this is the word he uses. The singular is *goy*, which is still used by some people nowadays as a jocular or derogatory slang word for a non-Jew.

But one of the most vivid Gospel stories to show Jesus' attitude to non-Jews is the account of his cure of the Syrophoenician woman's daughter. When she approached Jesus, and fell at his feet, imploring his help, Jesus is reported to have replied:

Let the children eat their fill first; for it is not good to take the children's bread and throw it to the little dogs.

By 'the children', Jesus meant his fellow Jews, and by 'the little dogs', he meant the rest of the human race — the *goyim*, or Gentiles. But the pagan woman in reply made a point of her own when she said, 'The little dogs under the table make a meal from the children's crumbs.'

Kamada So Jesus referred to non-Jews as 'dogs'?

Whitland If this story — which is in both Mark and Matthew — is true. And if Jesus spoke to the woman in his own language, he will have said quite simply 'dogs', because Aramaic had no word for 'puppy'. If he spoke to her in Greek, the word used in the Gospels still probably meant simply 'dogs', and not 'puppies' or even 'doggies' as some modern commentators would like to have it.

The editors of *The New Jerusalem Bible* apparently take this saying of the person they believe to be the Son of God made flesh to be authentic, and they comment on it, in all seriousness: 'Jesus' vocation is primarily to bring salvation to the Jews, "children" of God and of the promises, before caring for the Gentiles who were, in the eyes of the Jews, only "dogs". The conventional nature of this expression, and the diminutive form used in the Greek lessen the insult of it in Jesus' mouth.'

Kamada Yet they still feel that it was an insult! But I believe that you said earlier that there are other sayings in the Gospels that go against such a tribal, or racial view on Jesus' part.

Whitland Well, it could be argued, couldn't it, that Jesus' disavowal of the blood family excludes a tribal view of mankind's fate.

But actions speak louder than words, and in his conduct Jesus did not show what would nowadays be called a racist bias. I am thinking of the Samaritan leper he cured, while at the same time, if Luke is to be believed, referring to him as an 'allogen' — a foreigner.

Then there's that long and intimate conversation with the Samaritan woman at the well — and it is to her that he reveals himself explicitly as the promised Messiah.

Kamada In its origins, religion is usually tribal. Can we say that Jesus advanced the beliefs of his contemporaries beyond that stage?

Whitland I believe that before Jesus, some Jews were already looking for individual salvation rather than for the triumph of the Jews as a nation. Perhaps you can see the beginning of that in the Old Testament prophet Daniel, about 150 years before Jesus was born.

But it seems to me that Jesus, in his deeds and words, focused more sharply on the individual than any Jewish teacher before him. I referred to the Samaritan leper just now, but I don't think I mentioned the fact that he was the only one of ten lepers to thank Jesus for curing him. There you see a dramatic emphasis on the individual. And the parable of the lost sheep is also characteristic of his teaching:

> *If a man has one hundred sheep, and one of them wanders off, won't he leave the ninety-nine, and walk up the mountain, and look for the stray? And if it happens that he finds it, I tell you truly, he has more joy in that one than in the ninety-nine that did not stray.*

This strikes me as the authentic voice of Jesus.

Kamada But that is your personal feeling, isn't it?

Whitland Yes, but at the same time, the individual is, in a sense, defined by his membership of a tribe, in the case of the leper, or a flock, in the parable of the lost sheep. So, as usual, the matter is not so simple.

Chapter 29

Jesus cures a woman with a haemorrhage

Kamada You spoke yesterday about Jesus curing the daughter of the Syrophoenician woman. Was this a miraculous cure?

Whitland I think the girl's illness is not specified — she was possessed by an unclean spirit, which was a general way of describing illness then, just as today we might talk of someone picking up a bug.

Hiraoka A bug?

Whitland A germ, or a virus. But according to the Gospels, Jesus did not go to the child — he cured her at a distance, as a reward for her mother's remark about the dogs under the table eating the crumbs. He seems to have liked that reply. This was not the only miracle that Jesus performed at a distance, but it is remarkable, if only for that reason.

Hiraoka And this was not the only female that Jesus cured?

Whitland Certainly not. In fact, if I remember rightly, one of his earliest miracles was curing his disciple Simon's mother-in-law of a fever.

Kamada That does not sound so miraculous.
Whitland No, but the story may interest Dr Hiraoka, because this

woman is the only woman to be identified as someone's mother-in-law in the Gospels, and perhaps for this reason she has become a stock figure in Greek folk tales — usually depicted as something of a shrew.

Hiraoka I did not know that Jesus had disciples who were married.

Whitland I believe this is the only reference to a married disciple. You know, the more I read the Gospels, the more the impression grows on me that the disciples were teenagers, rather than the dignified, usually bearded men portrayed in Christian art. I cannot point to anything specific — it simply seems to fit their behaviour and what they say on certain occasions.

Kamada I certainly see nothing very improbable in what you say.

Whitland In any case, Simon is the only disciple on record as a married man. Jesus later gave Simon the name, or nickname, Kepha, which means 'Rock' in Aramaic, and it is through the Greek translation of this word as *Petros* that Simon has became better known, as Peter in English, Pierre in French, and so on.

But I think Dr Hiraoka may find it more significant for her research that as soon as the good lady, Simon's mother-in-law I mean, had been cured of her fever, she evidently got going with the housework.

Hiraoka [*With apologies to Whitland, exchanges a few words with Professor Kamada in Japanese.*]

Kamada Yes, we should be interested to know whether there are reports in the Gospels of Jesus curing specifically gynaecological diseases.

Whitland I should have to ask a gynaecologist! But perhaps Jesus' cure of the woman with a haemorrhage, which all three narrative Gospels report, comes into this category, as it has been suggested that this was a continuous uterine haemorrhage. One interesting point about this cure is that it is the only specific example in the Gospels of an involuntary miracle on Jesus' part, although there are general allusions to people being saved simply by touching him.

In Mark's version of the incident, which is more detailed than either Matthew's or Luke's, the woman had been suffering for twelve years, and had had a tough time at the hands of several doctors. She had spent all her money, but to no avail. In fact, she had got worse. She had heard about Jesus, says Mark, and came up behind him in the crowd, and touched his cloak:

> *Because she thought, 'Even if I only touch his clothes, I shall be saved.' And immediately the source of the blood dried up, and she knew in her body that she was cured of her affliction. And immediately Jesus, aware in himself of the power going out of him, turned round in the crowd and said: 'Who touched my clothes?' And his disciples said to him, 'You see the crowd squashing you, and you say, "Who touched me?"' And he went on looking round to see who had done this. And the woman, in fear and trembling when she realised what had happened to her, came and fell at his feet and told him the whole truth.*
>
> *And he told her, 'Daughter, your faith has saved you. Go in peace, and be cured of your affliction.'*

Hiraoka Has saved you? Please, I do not understand.

Whitland Well, it's true that for some commentators, the woman's statement, 'I shall be saved', and Jesus' remark to her have a significance beyond the medical. But other scholars maintain that the word 'saved' simply means 'cured' here.

In other words, it is doubtful whether she was making the theological statement attributed to her by one modern biblical scholar who claims 'the woman relied on the life and work of Jesus recognised as the saving power of God active in the world'. I can only say that my own impression of the story, as told by Mark, is that it indicates no more than the woman's naive belief in Jesus' healing power.

Kamada Yes, the woman evidently believed in a power that could flow unseen from Jesus, rather like electricity. And it is also interesting that Jesus himself is reported to have felt something like a loss of power.

Whitland The belief in a power of this kind was not uncommon in antiquity, and for that matter is still fairly widespread today. Luke describes 'a whole crowd' trying to touch Jesus, 'because power went out from him and cured them all'. The word for 'power' in all these contexts is *dunamis*.

Hiraoka Why was the woman in fear and trembling?

Whitland Perhaps because she felt she had been supernaturally cured, or perhaps because Jesus looked at her in a fear-inspiring way.

Hiraoka It's possible.

Whitland But since, according to traditional Jewish belief, a woman with this complaint would be lacking cleanliness and pollute anything that she came into contact with, the woman may have been terrified on this score.

The three Gospel writers agree that the woman had been ill for twelve years, and perhaps the number is chosen for its symbolic force. It may not be by chance that all three Gospels place the incident in the same context, interrupting the story of a miraculous cure of a girl aged twelve. And Luke, having told this girl's story, continues immediately, 'He called the Twelve together...' — the twelve disciples, who symbolically represented the twelve original tribes of Israel.

Hiraoka You said, didn't you, that Jesus called the woman 'Daughter'.

Whitland Yes, although she was evidently his age, or even older, and it is the only time in the Gospels that he addresses a woman in this way — perhaps he wanted to emphasise the fact that he did not regard her as a person who would pollute him.

There may be some other significance in this form of address that eludes us. On another occasion, Jesus referred to a woman he had cured as a daughter of Abraham.

Hiraoka Please — I should like to hear more about this woman.

Whitland Luke is the only Gospel writer to report the miraculous cure of a woman who had been bent double for eighteen years and was altogether unable to lift her head up. Jesus, he says, saw her in the synagogue and called out to her and said: 'Woman, you are freed from your disability,' and he placed his hands on her, and she immediately straightened up and praised God.

At this, the head of the synagogue was greatly annoyed, because it was the Jewish holy day, the Sabbath, and he told the crowd in the synagogue to come and be cured on one of the six working days of the week, but not on the Sabbath.

Jesus then rounded on him with a charge of hypocrisy, saying that everyone led his ox or his donkey out to drink on the Sabbath, 'and this woman, a daughter of Abraham whom Satan kept bound for eighteen years ought not to be set free from this bond on the Sabbath day?'

Kamada Usually in the Gospels, nameless demons are spoken of as the cause of disease, but here we have Satan, the evil power opposed to God in Jewish belief — he is not a demon like the others.

Whitland No, he is not a minor demon. He is the one and only Devil, and although his role in the cosmic scheme of things develops in the course of time, his existence does eventually lend itself to a dualistic creed.

On a less weighty matter, however, I should like to say that the mention of the 'eighteen years' during which this woman was afflicted is typical of the individual detail with which Luke likes to adorn a tale. But the point of the story is this matter of the Sabbath, which according to one commentator 'was a weekly foretaste of the rest which awaited the people of God in the kingdom, the final release from all bondage'.

The miracle is also unusual, however, in that the woman is not reported as professing a belief in Jesus, and neither does Jesus say anything about her sins being forgiven.

Chapter 30

❧

Mary Magdalene's seven demons

Kamada You told us this morning about two miraculous cures of afflicted women. Are there any more miracles of this kind reported in the Gospels?

Whitland Yes, but not in such detail. There is the passage at the beginning of the eighth chapter of Luke's Gospel that Carla Ricci has made the starting-point and the dominant theme of her book about Mary Magdalene and the many other women who were followers of Jesus:

> Jesus journeyed through towns and villages, publicly announcing the good news of the kingdom of God, and the twelve were with him, and some women who had been cured of evil spirits and illnesses, Mary known as the woman from Magdala, from whom seven demons had gone out, and Joanna the wife of Herod's household manager Chuza, Susanna, and many others, who provided for them out of their own resources.

That strikes me as a passage that withholds more information than it imparts.

Kamada Herod was the king...

Whitland Yes, the puppet ruler, under the Romans, of Galilee. He was the king who had Jesus' cousin, John the Baptist, beheaded at

Salome's request.

Joanna is mentioned again by Luke as one of the women who saw the two men in brilliant clothes who appeared at Jesus' tomb, and, by implication, as one of the women who followed Jesus from Galilee to his crucifixion at Golgotha, the so-called 'Place of the Skull' outside the city walls of Jerusalem.

It is curious that nothing more is said by Luke about Joanna — a woman who, as Carla Ricci points out, must have left her husband, unless she was a widow, and the royal court to follow Jesus.

As for Susanna, this is the only mention of her in the Gospels, which supports Carla Ricci's argument that there is a conspiracy of silence about these women.

I think it would be true to say that most Christians, if they think about it, picture Jesus as wandering about Palestine in the company of his twelve male disciples. Yet, according to Luke, there were many other women in his entourage. According to the conventions of the time, it would have been most unusual — probably altogether unheard of — for a rabbi, a religious teacher, to have been accompanied on his travels by a crowd of women.

Kamada Were both the women and Jesus himself, then, behaving in an unprecedented way?

Whitland Yes, I should say that they both were. It has been suggested, too, that in Jesus' case, his conduct must have seemed even more extraordinary in view of the fact that some of these women would have been regarded by most people at the time as social outcasts. That, at any rate, seems to be implied by their having been cured of evil spirits.

Hiraoka *Wakarimasen!* Excuse me... What made these women leave home and follow Jesus on his travels? Had they all been ill? And had Jesus cured them all?

Whitland I think the Gospel text is not absolutely clear about that. But the most likely answer to your question is 'yes' — at least as far as the women who are named here by Luke are concerned.

Hiraoka And what is meant by 'seven demons'?

Whitland No one knows, although many people have tried to guess what they mean, and these guesses tend to reflect the medical fashions prevalent in the time of the person making the guess. So nowadays, the most common explanation of the seven demons is that they represent some kind of psychological or, should I say, psychosomatic disorder.

The number seven had — and still has — special connotations, and in this context can be taken to imply that whatever Mary Magdalene's illness was, it was regarded by her and those who came into contact with her as serious. Indeed, Jesus himself seems to have regarded seven demons as especially malignant carriers of disease, when he threatened 'this evil generation' with an attack by them

But although next to nothing is said in the Gospels about all these women who had been cured by Jesus, I should imagine that the fact that they had all, so to speak, upped sticks to follow him means that none of them had been suffering from a merely minor ailment.

Kamada All the same, these women surely testify to something compelling in Jesus' personality.

Whitland To say the least! In fact, all four Gospels preserve the tradition that he had only to call people — even, apparently, complete strangers — and they dropped whatever they were doing, and followed him.

Chapter 31

⤦

The widow who would give a judge a black eye

Kamada The last time we met, you referred to the possibility that one of the women who followed Jesus was a widow. It would be interesting to hear what the Gospels say about Jesus' attitude towards widows. Dr Hiraoka thinks that he had a special sympathy for widows.

Whitland Well, to begin with, I believe that there are more than twice as many references to widows in Luke's Gospel as in the other three Gospels put together. So it may be Luke rather than Jesus who had a special sympathy for widows. Another point is that there were relatively more of them in his time than there are nowadays.

It is difficult to be certain about any demographic data in New Testament times, but there is anecdotal evidence of long widowhoods — we must suppose that many girls were married to much older men, especially as at that time men lived longer on average than women.

As Christianity established itself as a religion distinct from mainstream Judaism, widows were numerically important. Four hundred years after Jesus' time, the church at Antioch — the first Christian church to be built — supported three thousand widows and virgins.

Hiraoka I have heard it suggested that one reason why Christianity prevailed against rival cults was the welfare support that the church offered to persons in need. Without help of that kind, the condition of most widows would have been extremely wretched.

Whitland Yes. What made things particularly bad for them was their low status in the eyes of the law. Jesus referred specifically to this, when he issued a warning against learned lawyers who liked to walk about in long robes, be recognised ceremoniously in public, and bag the best seats in the synagogue and at banquets. These are the very men, said Jesus, who devour the property of widows, and at the same time make a show of saying long prayers. 'All the stiffer the sentence they'll get,' he adds.

One scholar holds that these lawyers were legal managers of rich widows' estates, and were taking inordinately high fees for doing so. But it is not difficult to imagine quite poor widows falling victim to them,as well.

A more cheerful note is struck, however, in the story Jesus told his disciples about a widow who kept pestering a judge.

Hiraoka The story? It was not one of his encounters?

Whitland No, it was a parable. Jesus had just been urging his disciples to pray continually and not slacken their efforts. To make his point more vividly, he told them this anecdote:

> There was a judge in some town or other, who was not afraid of God and had no time for the human race. There was also a widow in that town who kept coming to him and saying, 'I have an enemy, and I want you to help me get even with him.' For a long time, the judge did not want to listen to her. But then he said to himself, 'Even if I'm not afraid of God and have no time for my fellow men, because this widow is being such a bore, I shall give her satisfaction. Otherwise, she might come and give me a black eye.'

Kamada A black eye!

Whitland Yes. I admit that I've just translated this parable from Luke's

Gospel rather freely, but I've kept the sense of the original, all the same. Some modern translators don't seem to find Luke's language dignified enough, especially the bit about the black eye. 'Her continual visits will be the death of me!' says one, and 'before she wears me out with her persistence' says another. But the word here in Luke really does mean 'to hit under the eye; to give someone a black eye'.

Jesus went on to draw the moral from this story — that God would also see justice done on behalf of those he had chosen, if they kept calling to him day and night.

Kamada This story of the obstreperous widow perhaps contains a grain of humour, but as a parable — an analogy — it does not quite hold. Even metaphorically speaking, the God of the Gospels can hardly be afraid of getting a black eye from one of his creatures, even though he may be bothered by them.

Whitland Well, then! In that case, the bit about the black eye really was meant as a joke. But there's another story about a widow, which may refer to an actual incident that Jesus witnessed, or again, may have originally been a parable.

This is the story of a widow who was a beggar. Jesus saw her put a couple of small coins into the collecting box in the temple in Jerusalem. A lot of rich people were putting large sums of money into the box, but Jesus called his disciples, and told them:

This poor widow has put more than all the others into the collecting box. Because what they all put in was their surplus cash, but she put in money that she really needed, everything she had, all she had to live on.

You will not find this widow described as a beggar in any of the translations, but that is how she is described by Mark, and the fact that she was a beggar explains how Jesus was able to tell that the couple of farthings she put in the collecting box were all her worldly fortune.

Some commentators have found this insight of Jesus a problem, and a leading German authority on the Gospels apparently thought there was something supernatural about it. Others, as I just hinted, have supposed that this story started life as a parable told by Jesus, in which case he could claim the usual omniscience of an author about one of his characters. But if Mark is describing an actual incident, we have only to suppose that Jesus was showing a bit of imagination, or indulging in exaggeration — something he was apt to do.

Kamada Whatever the true origin of this episode, there is certainly no need to labour the story's moral. But it may perhaps strike Dr Hiraoka as significant that Jesus chose a woman, more specifically a widow, as his model of self-denying generosity.

Whitland There are other widows in the Gospels. But I believe that only one of them is named, and that is Anna. According to Luke, she had been widowed 'after seven years from her virginity', and, at the age of 84, had never left the Temple, where she worshipped day and night with fasting and prayers.

When Joseph and Mary took the new-born baby Jesus to be presented to God as 'the male child who opened the womb', Anna appeared and began to return thanks to God, and she spoke about the child 'to all who were waiting for the ransoming of Jerusalem' — by 'ransoming' Luke means the freeing of Jerusalem by the long-awaited Messiah.

Luke calls Anna a prophetess — a woman dedicated to God and able to interpret him to ordinary folk. He is specific in identifying her as the daughter of Phanuel, a member of the tribe of Asher, who is not otherwise mentioned in the Gospels. But Luke's is the only Gospel to relate Anna's encounter with the infant Jesus.

Chapter 32

⸙

Jesus brings a widow's dead son back to life

Kamada Since we last met, Dr Hiraoka has been looking further into the Gospel stories about widows. She has been impressed by a remarkable miracle, which only Mark...

Hiraoka *Chotto shitsurei shimasu!* Only Luke...

Kamada Yes! The story is only in Luke's Gospel. He tells how Jesus raised a widow's dead son to life.

Hiraoka Yes, he was a young man who had died. But the emphasis of the story, it seems to me, is on the young man's mother, the widow. It is the mother who concerns Jesus, the mother who excites his compassion.

Whitland Let me see... It is in Luke. Yes, here we are:

> *Jesus went on his way to a town called Naïn; and his disciples walked along with him, as did a large crowd. As he approached the gate of the town, lo and behold, a dead man was being carried out, his mother's only son, and she was a widow; and there was quite a crowd from the town with her.*
>
> *When Jesus saw her, he felt pity for her, and he told her: 'Don't cry.'*

Then he stepped forward and touched the stand that carried the corpse, and the men carrying it stood still. And he said, 'Young man, I tell you, wake up!'

And the dead man sat up and began to talk, and Jesus gave him to his mother. They were all terrified, and they glorified God, saying that a great prophet had arisen among them, and that God had visited his people. And this account of him spread throughout Judaea and the surrounding country.

Yes, Dr Hiraoka, you are right. The focus of Luke's narrative is the plight of the widow. But I have to admit it had never struck me.

Kamada This is, perhaps, the difference between a man's reading of the story and a woman's. But what are we to make of such a miracle?

Whitland In the Gospels, we read that Jesus brought three dead people back to life. There is this young man, the widow's son, and there is the resuscitation of the twelve-year-old daughter of a synagogue leader, although in her case there is a suggestion, at least, that she was not really dead, but simply in a coma.

But I suppose the most famous resurrection wrought by Jesus is the raising of Lazarus, the brother of Mary and Martha. Perhaps this is because Lazarus had been dead four days, and was already stinking.

It is true that these miracles pose problems for present-day readers, and even in Jesus' lifetime, the question whether the dead could be brought back to life or not was hotly debated among the Jews. The majority of people, however, believed that they could.

Jesus himself emphatically and unambiguously stated his own belief in the resurrection of the dead. I'm thinking of his reply to the riddle about the seven brothers who successively married the same repeatedly widowed woman. It's true that Jesus may have understood resurrection in an immaterial way, as he compared the risen dead to angels, who were, I suppose, spiritual rather than physical beings. But it is not until after Jesus' death that his followers developed the notion that 'what is saved at resurrection is a spiritual body'.

In a more direct way, in fact, according to Luke, Jesus claimed that the dead had been raised, when he sent a message to his cousin, John the Baptist, listing the miracles that he had performed.

Then there is also the saying about entering the Kingdom of God with only one foot or only one eye that, if taken literally, as surely some of Jesus' audience would have taken it, does suggest a physical survival.

Kamada It would be interesting to trace the history of this idea that dead bodies could come back to life again.

Whitland I have read somewhere that this belief originated with the ancient Persians, and became known to the Hebrews during their exile to Babylon in the sixth century BC In any event, it was a rather late arrival in their history, though by the time the Gospels were written, it was accepted fairly generally, as many texts show. And what I think is the most astonishing description of dead men rising bodily from their tombs is to be found in Matthew's report on the natural calamities that accompanied Jesus' death on the cross:

> The veil of the Temple was split in two from top to bottom, there was an earthquake, the rocks were split, and the tombs were opened, and many bodies of saints who had been sleeping rose up, and they came out of their tombs after his awaking from death and entered the holy city, and made their appearance to many people.

Kamada But have I understood you rightly? Did you say that this question — whether dead bodies stood up again or not — was still the subject of dispute among Jews in Jesus' own time?

Whitland Yes, that is so.

Kamada If many bodies rose up in the way you have just described and appeared to many people, surely one would have expected that to have settled the argument.

Whitland Yes, you certainly might think so. But from at least one passage later in the New Testament, we know that it did not.

We know, too, that in the early years of the religion, even pious Christians had difficulties in taking this account of the mass rising of dead saints at Jerusalem at its face value. One modern theologian calls it 'a Matthean *midrashic* gloss in paratactic style'.

Kamada That seems to be explaining one riddle by another. What is a *midrashic* gloss?

Whitland The *midrash* is an early commentary on the Hebrew scriptures. But when critical methods were first applied to the explanation of the Gospels, some commentators expressed their surprise at the fact that these remarkable events were not mentioned by any ancient secular historian. To many scholars, it seems likely that Matthew was inspired to write these verses about the mass rising of dead saints by some lurid passages in the Old Testament rather than by actual events in Jerusalem.

And another remarkable event reported in the Old Testament story may also be Luke's real source for the story about the raising of the widow's son at Naïn. This is the incident where the prophet Elijah, who lived more than 800 years before Jesus, visits the town of Zarephath (in what is now Lebanon), and brings a widow's son back to life. By what may be more than a mere coincidence, Luke refers to this same visit to Zarephath a few chapters before his account of the miracle at Naïn.

One more curious point is that the town of Naïn is never mentioned in the New Testament apart from in this story in Luke. And modern scholarship has shown that Luke has not only invented some parts of his Gospel, but was capable of disservice to the truth by omission.

Kamada It is difficult, then, to avoid the conclusion that what really happened at Naïn on this occasion will never be established. But are Christians required to take Luke's account literally — to believe that this and the other miracles of restoring the dead to life were actually accomplished by Jesus?

Whitland Some Christians are required by their Church to believe in miracles. But as far as I know, the only resurrection of a specific individual that all Christians have to affirm outright — which they do in their formal statement of belief known as the Creed — is the resurrection of Jesus himself.

The Creeds of all the churches affirm a general rising again of human beings 'with their bodies' or 'in the flesh' — but this seems to be a future event, perhaps entailing the simultaneous resurrection of the whole human race when this world comes to an end. For good measure, the Creed of the fourth-century Saint Athanasius, recited by Church of England congregations on certain feast days, adds: 'And they that have done good shall go into life everlasting: and they that have done evil into everlasting fire.'

Kamada That assertion of eternal punishment, again!

Whitland But whatever the various churches may teach about the resurrection of the flesh, if we consider this miracle at Naïn, I think we would be hard put to it to find a modern commentator on the Gospels who is ready to say in as many words: 'Yes. This actually happened. The widow's son was dead, and Jesus brought him back to life again.'

The drift of the various modern commentaries on this miracle is that it was regarded by Luke as the fulfilment of a prophecy; that the early Christians were convinced this miracle happened as Luke describes it; or that, as Dr George Caird puts it, 'The resuscitation of the dead is as well attested as any of the other miracles of Jesus.'

Kamada But that falls short of a clear endorsement of Luke's text. And what do these commentators say about the resurrection of Jesus, as it is described in the Gospels?

Whitland Many of them seem wary of committing themselves. Graham Stanton, who holds the chair of New Testament Studies at King's College, London, sums up neatly what other theologians some-times take thousands of words to express: 'For the Christian today, resurrection faith rests on the experiences of the disciples, on the reality of which the historian can say little.'

One historian I believe I have already mentioned — Professor E. P. Sanders — seems to recognise this when he writes, 'Something happened to the followers of Jesus, but we do not know what it was.'

Kamada Yet that 'something' is the basis of the Christian religion! From what you have told us, it seems that the idea of corpses coming back to life was one that presented no difficulties to Jesus' disciples.

Whitland No insuperable difficulties, anyway.

Kamada Well, at the end of the world, they expected everyone to rise from the dead, and in the meantime, the occasional resurrection — even of a number of corpses simultaneously — was possible, though perhaps unusual.

It was not, perhaps, something that occurred every day of the week, but it could happen. To me, this is an important presupposition to the story of

Jesus' own resurrection after the crucifixion, and I should like to ask you if the modern authorities you quoted consider the problem in this light.

Whitland No, I do not recall them approaching the question from this angle.

Kamada But to say the least, there is an important culturally determined element in this central tenet of Christianity.

Whitland In general, Christian theologians are aware, of course, that the Jewish scriptures and the commentaries on them did create the framework of beliefs and expectations that made the emergence of Christianity possible.

Kamada In general... But more specifically, a religion established on the belief that its founder rose from the dead on the third day after his execution could come into existence only in a culture that took resurrection for granted.

Whitland I am not sure, however, in what sense Jesus' disciples could be said to have taken resurrection for granted. According to Professor Sanders, 'The early Christians wished to affirm a bodily resurrection, but not a renewal of Jesus' physical life.'

A contemporary Roman Catholic theologian, Professor Hans Küng, seems to say something similar when he claims that 'The followers of the crucified Jesus of Nazareth never presented the resurrection of Jesus as the miracle of raising a dead person to this life.' Küng is not the most lucid of apologists for Christianity, but when he finally spells out 'what "resurrection" does and does not mean', he says quite plainly that it does not mean a return to life in this space and time, 'but a new life which bursts the dimensions of space and time, new life in God's invisible, incomprehensible sphere, symbolically called "heaven"'.

Kamada Yet although this sphere is incomprehensible, Professor Küng still manages to write about it! His interpretation of the resurrection is certainly not easy to grasp, but neither is Professor Sanders' reference to a bodily resurrection that is not physical.

Whitland Yes, especially in the light of Luke's statement that after the crucifixion, and after his body had disappeared from the tomb, Jesus appeared to the disciples in Jerusalem and asked them whether they had anything to hand to eat, whereupon they offered him a slice of baked fish, which he took and ate in front of them.

Chapter 33

⌒

Jesus in the Garden of Nature

Whitland It is sad that this is our last meeting — this year, at least. Because, as you know, I am hoping to return next year.

Kamada Yes. We also mean to say *dewa mata*, rather than *sayonara*...

Whitland So we shan't dwell on that... But I must tell you that I came here yesterday evening at twilight, to say farewell to this wonderful garden. You know, I think I shall miss its sounds more than its sights — I mean the humming of the insects, the bird-song, and above all, the delightful sound of the water streaming over the rocks.

Kamada We call it 'the Garden of Shizen' — that's to say, 'the Garden of Nature', so it is right to pay your respects to the insects and birds. But the waterfall was built by our gardeners, so there is also an element of art in those sounds.

Whitland It has been said that neither nature alone nor art alone can contrive anything as beautiful. But there is an ancient view that nature itself is an artist, possessed of a skill that no human craft or handiwork can rival — indeed, this view is echoed in the Gospels when Jesus speaks of the beauty of the flowers of the field.

Kamada We Japanese, at any rate, do regard nature as autonomous. The word *shizen* means, literally, 'self-created'.

Whitland There is a parallel to that in the attempts of some ancient Greek philosophers to define nature, when they called it a self-moved condition or system.

Kamada But how is nature defined in the Gospels?

Whitland It is not defined.

Kamada But if by nature we mean the world of plant and animal life that surrounds us and of which we, too, are part, admittedly a problematic part, then the Gospel writers — and Jesus himself — must surely have had some fundamental notions about it. We have seen, for example, that in their view it was a world, wasn't it, where all sorts of miracles could happen.

Whitland In using the word 'miracle' in that way, you are also, if I may say so, yourself carrying some culturally determined intellectual luggage!

As there has been so much discussion, throughout the centuries, of the miracles reported in both the Old Testament and the New Testament, perhaps I may remark that neither in ancient Hebrew nor in the Greek of the Gospels is there a specific word for 'miracle'.

By that, I mean that there is no word dedicated to meaning a violation or overriding of the order of nature — and that, I take it, is what we always mean nowadays when we speak of a miracle. In both the Old Testament and the New Testament, when what we regard as miracles occur, they are described as 'signs' or 'portents' or 'wonders' or 'acts of power'.

Kamada But if this is so, the reason must be that the ancient Jews lacked a properly developed idea of the order of nature. In other words, there was for them no order to be violated.

Whitland Indeed, it could be said that they regarded everything in nature as miraculous in the loose sense.

Kamada Then let us look at these natural phenomena as they are described in the Gospels, even if there is, as you say, no definition there of nature as such, and even if the Jews of Jesus' time regarded everything in nature with marvel.

Whitland Well, we must even be careful in talking about natural phenomena in the context of the Gospels. The ancient Greeks, of course, had a word for 'nature', which, like the English word, had several related meanings. And the word 'phenomena' is itself Greek, and sometimes used by ancient Greek writers in ways very much like the ways in which we use it.

But the Greek word for nature — *phusis* — does not occur in the Gospels, and perhaps this is not surprising, in view of the fact that Jesus' native language — Aramaic — had no expression corresponding to this Greek word. For the ancient Jews, the world was the work of God, and he was still at work in it. The signs or wonders or acts of power that we tend to label 'miracles' were, in their eyes, acts of intervention by God in the world he had created, where he could break the apparent rules or regularities, because he had made the rules in the first place.

Kamada No word for 'miracle', no word for 'nature' — this is no mere coincidence! But of course, Jesus had some notions on the subject. Even if he had no conception of laws of nature, he surely was aware of certain regularities — the 'apparent rules' that you have just referred to — in the natural world.

Whitland Well, according to Matthew, he once asked his listeners, ironically, whether grapes could be picked from thorns or figs from thistles.

Kamada That doesn't take us very far!

Whitland He refers, also, to the fig tree in leaf as a sign that summer is near. Nature, however, also contains irregularities or apparent irregularities, at least, and I think that this is implied in Jesus' remark, in John's Gospel, that the wind blows where it wants to.

But it has been claimed by some commentators that Jesus was something of a bookworm, rather than a keenly interested observer of the countryside and the work of farmers or fishermen.

For example, in his very interesting book about Jesus, A. N. Wilson comments on the strange behaviour of the sower, sowing his seed, in one of Jesus' most famous parables. No one, he points out, apart from an obscure German scholar earlier in this century, has ever seen a farmer randomly scattering seed on unploughed land and expecting it to grow, in the way that Jesus describes.

There are, it appears, other rather startling gaps in Jesus' knowledge of the natural world — or misunderstandings derived from legal text books he had read. One very curious story in this respect is Mark's account of the fig tree that Jesus cursed.

Hiraoka I am not sure that I remember this story.

Whitland Jesus had been staying overnight in the town of Bethany with his disciples, and as they were leaving the village, says Mark,

> *He was hungry. And seeing a fig tree in leaf in the distance, he went to see if he could find anything on it. And when he came to the tree, he found nothing but leaves, because it was not the season for figs.*

216

> *And answering the tree, he said to it, 'May no one ever eat fruit from*
> *you again.' And his disciples heard him.*

Now, isn't it strange that Jesus, who could refer to fig trees in leaf as a presage of summer, was not aware that figs weren't in season at this moment when he cursed the fig tree?

Hiraoka It is strange! But did the curse work?

Whitland Yes, apparently it did. Because, again according to Mark:

> *Passing by the next morning, they saw that the fig tree was withered*
> *from its roots up. And Peter remembered, and says to him, 'Rabbi,*
> *look! The fig tree that you cursed has withered.'*

Jesus' reply to this is also strange. He claims the miracle as a demonstration of faith in God, and says that in the same way, a man with utterly unquestioning faith could order a mountain to uproot itself and throw itself into the sea, and it would happen.

But the cursing of the fig tree is, after all, a negative miracle — according to Professor Stanton, it is the only destructive miracle in the Gospels, although some of the two thousand pigs that Jesus caused to plunge from a cliff and drown in the Sea of Galilee may have had a different view about that.

But of course, Christian commentators have attempted to make sense of the whole episode of the withered fig tree.

'Jesus meant to perform a symbolic action,' say the editors of *The New Jerusalem Bible*, and they refer to a passage in the Old Testament to support their interpretation whereby the fig tree represents Israel, 'punished for its fruitlessness'. It has also been suggested that the story is an elaboration of a parable recorded by Luke, rather than an account of something that actually happened.

Kamada A confusion of this kind, between parable and actual incident, would arise easily in the conditions of the time.

Whitland Even today, you can find analogous confusion — for instance, purely fictional characters in television soap operas are taken by many viewers to be real people.

But I think that Jesus and his fellow Jews simply had no philosophical or scientific interest in the natural world, such as the ancient Greeks had, for instance. Indeed, it has been said of the early Christians that they made no effort to understand the world of nature until they gradually became aware that the world was not going to come to an end at any minute, but was likely to last a long time.

So what we think of as nature, whether red in tooth and claw, or as a scene of beauty or as providential supply of our wants, is for Jesus no more than either a source of metaphor or image, to illustrate his teaching, or a stage for his miracles.

Kamada You have just spoken of nature as red in tooth and claw — something, I know, that has troubled many western thinkers who would like to believe in a creator god who is both omnipotent and beneficent. Does Jesus have any conception of this aspect of nature?

Whitland Well, he certainly knows nothing of the ichneumon wasp.

Hiraoka *Mo ichido* — please, you mean...

Whitland The insect who lays her egg in a caterpillar, so that her larva can feed on it, and purposefully stings each ganglion of the caterpillar's central nervous system, so as to paralyse it but not kill it.

Kamada Purposefully?

Whitland Yes, so we are told. As the Oxford zoologist Richard Dawkins puts it, 'this way the meat keeps fresh'.

He adds that we do not know whether the paralysis acts as a general anaesthetic, or if it merely freezes the victim's ability to move. In that case, the prey might be aware of being eaten alive from inside, but unable to move a muscle to do anything about it.

Hiraoka Yes, there is cruelty in nature.

Whitland Not according to Professor Dawkins. He says nature is not cruel, only pitilessly indifferent.

Jesus himself refers to the neutrality, as it were, of nature when, according to Matthew, he says, 'Your Father in heaven makes his sun rise on evil people and on good, and he sends rain to wicked people as well as to good.'

Kamada This is a beneficent neutrality, not pitiless indifference!

Whitland Certainly! Jesus was speaking here about God's indiscriminate love for his creatures. And, as far as we can tell from the Gospels, Jesus did not seem to regard the natural world as an arena of suffering — on the contrary, he claims that foxes and birds are better housed than he is, and that God doesn't forget a single sparrow falling off the twig.

On the other hand, Jesus knows about wolves and poisonous snakes and scorpions...

Kamada Yes, his picture of the natural world includes some of its horrors. I think you told us that he mentions earthquakes as symptoms of this world's destruction.

Whitland Yes, if the Gospels really do record his actual words. He also talks of floods and of a river bursting its banks. But of course, Jesus

219

never speaks as a naturalist or a meteorologist! His preaching is about the world of the spirit.

Kamada The world of the supernatural?

Whitland Not really. It is more the case that he did not make a sharp distinction between what we think of as the natural world and what some people would regard as the sphere of the supernatural. His natural world was crowded with many beings that we would think of as supernatural — angels, for example, and evil spirits.

Kamada But surely the miracles are miraculous — the signs are significant — only because they are exceptional deeds from the point of view of our everyday experience of nature.

Whitland Especially the so-called 'nature miracles'!

Hiraoka The nature miracles?

Whitland Such as walking on water, or feeding five thousand men and an unspecified number of women and children with five loaves and two fishes. Because some modern commentators have found it convenient to treat them as a separate category from Jesus' healing miracles.

Kamada They may do that, if they like. But there is no fundamental distinction between the two categories — they both overturn the way things usually happen!

Whitland Yet as far as I can understand these writers, they seem to say that the healing miracles could have happened, or did happen, whereas the nature miracles reflect the Gospel writers' intention to present Jesus as the Messiah — they attribute them to what these modern writers call 'christology' rather than, so to speak, to a genuinely historical record.

As an example of this line of argument, I could mention Jesus' miracle of turning the water into wine at the wedding party in Cana. One commentator says we have to ask whether John, who relates this miracle, intended such a story to be taken literally. And another explains that, 'The glory of Jesus which is revealed in this story is not the power to change water into wine, but to give eternal life.'

Kamada But then I have to ask, if these stories are mere metaphors, why do they contain realistic detail? I seem to remember your telling us that the actual quantity of wine is specified by John, and the object of giving such detail is usually to reinforce a story's claim to be actual, to be true.

Whitland I believe I also told you that the story of the water turned into wine is told by John in a style reminiscent of folk tales. And with this in mind, I should add that there were several stories of this kind circulating in the eastern Mediterranean about the time of Jesus.

In the Aegean coastal town of Teos, for example — the present-day Seferihisar in Turkey — we're told by a Greek writer in the century before Jesus that a natural spring changed into wine at fixed intervals, to celebrate the birth of the god of wine there. And the Roman encyclopaedist Pliny, a contemporary of the three narrative Gospel writers, tells a similar story about water in the temple of the wine god on the Greek island of Andros, to the east of Athens.

Another Gospel miracle, which echoes stories reported by pagan writers, although they often challenge their truth, is the miracle of Jesus walking on water.

Kamada Then these so-called nature miracle stories are also culturally determined... Could one say that they are part of Jewish folklore?

Whitland Perhaps they derive from Greek sources, rather than Jewish. Mark's Gospel has been particularly singled out from this point of view, but one of the most striking stories of this kind is told by Matthew, and only by Matthew.

He says that when the collectors of the Temple tax approached Peter and asked for the payment due from Jesus, Jesus told Peter to go to the sea — the Lake of Galilee — and cast a hook, take the first fish to rise, open its mouth, and find the coin the tax collectors were demanding. 'Take it, and give it to them on my behalf and yours,' says Jesus.

There are several parallels to this story, say the editors of *The New Jerusalem Bible*, in Jewish and Greek folklore. Well, a story that springs immediately to mind is the one Herodotus tells about Polycrates, the dictator of the Greek island of Samos. An Egyptian advised Polycrates to throw a ring he valued into the sea, in order to avert misfortune. But a few days later, the ring turned up again in the belly of a fish that a fisherman presented to the dictator. Is there any Japanese folk tale with a similar incident?

Kamada We have stories of magical sea creatures — there is the folk tale of Shima no Ko or Urashima Taro, for instance. He was a fisherman who visited the *ryugu*, the sea-god's coral and crystal palace at the bottom of the ocean. But I cannot think offhand of a story exactly like the story of the coin in the fish's mouth.

Yet even in these fairy stories, however childish they may be, the order of nature is turned upside down in an important way. I mean that the story of the magical fish springs from the same view of the world that accommodates the resuscitation of the dead. It is a view of the world that ultimately denies a natural order, as we understand it, at least.

Whitland Yes, but in order to deny a natural order of things, you

have to admit its possibility, at least in principle. And I'm not sure that
this possibility occurred to Jesus, in the way that is implicit in your
argument. For him, nature was subjective. As I have said, he saw it as
a source of images, of examples — he even compares himself to a hen
at one point. He saw it as the setting for his parables, because fields
sown to seed, vineyards, mustard plants, fig trees and so on were all
things his audience could relate to immediately. And because this was
the world in which he lived, it was also the scene of his miracles.

But none of this made nature an object for him. And in fact, nature
did not begin to become objective in the modern, scientific sense for
mankind until centuries after Jesus' death — until the seventeenth
century, in fact.

Kamada But even if Jesus had no general conception of nature, either
to affirm or to deny it, he seems to have thought that the world of
nature would come to an end at any minute, and if he does not repu-
diate the natural world in as many words, at least it is not of primary
importance to him. Doesn't this come close to a denial of nature?

Whitland Well, I was told once that all religions are founded on a
denial.

Kamada All religions? It would be difficult to say.

Whitland Yes, but I was struck by a remark in one of Mishima's novels that the denial of *atman* — the denial of the 'self', that is to say —
is the essence of Buddhism.

Kamada Does Mishima say that? I think it could be said that the question of a self was meaningless to the Buddha, to Gotama, and there is
a tradition that he refused to answer a wandering yogi who asked him
whether there is a self or not. Gotama did not think in terms of being,

but of becoming, nor did he think in terms of an element or substance underlying the world we experience. He thought, if I may so express it, rather in terms of interrelated conditions.

So, by denying the *atman*, the Buddha is saying that there is no core substance in living creatures that you can identify as the soul, let alone as the immortal soul. Buddhism does not recognise this soul, which in this sense was perhaps invented by Plato, who was born 60 years after the Buddha's death.

But if the Gospels do not express an indiscriminate denial of the natural world, they do deny specifically two of its most powerful and pervasive manifestations: sex and death.

If you deny death, sex loses its primary, its essential purpose — to propagate life. And if you deny sex, there is no point in exacting or paying the price that mankind, and not only mankind, has to pay in order to propagate the species. So it seems to me that if you deny the reality of one of these phenomena, you inevitably have to deny the reality of the other.

Notes and references

Chapter 1 Procreation without sex

when God created Adam: OT Genesis 2:7.
to cultivate it and look after it: OT Genesis 2:15.
God put Adam into a deep sleep: OT Genesis 2:21.

one modern commentator: Dr Grace I. Emmerson, 'Women in ancient Israel', in *The World of Ancient Israel*, ed. R. E. Clements, Cambridge University Press, 1989, p. 390. Dr Emmerson quotes a learned American commentator to baffling mathematical effect: 'The creation of a man first and of woman last constitutes a ring composition whereby the two creatures are parallel.'

In a letter to *The Times* on 15 March 1997, Professor George Fink, FRSE, commented on the Genesis report 'of the first human clone' with the remark that the replacement of the male (Y) by an additional female (X) chromosome in the cells of the male-derived rib will have been such a trivial exercise for God that the author of Genesis thought that it was not worth recounting.

Jesus may have known some Greek: Graham N. Stanton, *The Gospels and Jesus*, Oxford University Press, 1989, p. 146 , writes: 'Jesus spoke and taught in Aramaic, but he almost certainly would have spoken some Greek.' Professor Stanton even considers whether Jesus ever went to a Greek theatre near his home village of Nazareth. He asks, 'Is this the origin of his repeated use of the term 'hypocrite', the primary meaning of which is "stage actor"?'

If the incident described in St John's Gospel (John 12.20-23), in which Jesus greets the news that some Greeks want to see him with the words 'the hour has arrived for the Son of Man to be glorified', is true, Jesus certainly understood the importance of Greek, whether he spoke it himself or not. In another verse of John's Gospel (7:35), some Jews who had heard Jesus foretell his imminent departure, are reported to have asked, 'Is he going to go to the Jewish settlements among the Greeks and teach the Greeks?'

There are some sayings attributed to Jesus in the Gospels that have a very Greek ring to them: for instance, his instructions to his disciples at Mark 6:8-9 to take nothing for their travels apart from a walking-stick — 'no bread, no wallet, no money in their belts; sandals; but only one coat' — faithfully echo the teaching of the Greek Cynic philosophers (a school founded by one of Socrates' pupils, whose most famous representative is Diogenes, the witty sourpuss reputed to have lived in a large earthenware tub in the sanctuary of the Mother of the Gods in Athens).

The encounter with the pagan woman (Mark 7:24-30; Matt. 15:21-28) also raises the question as to what language she and Jesus conversed in.

For the suggestion that Jesus taught in Greek, 'the world language of the time', or at least in a lingo that was half-Greek, half-Aramaic, see Joseph Huby SJ and Xavier Léon-Dufour SJ, *L'Evangile et les Evangiles*, Paris, Beauchesne, 1954, p. 57.

their religion is rooted in specific historical events: 'the Catholic Christian, reciting the creed, declares his faith to rest upon a particular event in history... this is Christian orthodoxy, both Catholic and Protestant' — Sir Edwyn Hoskyns and Noel Davey, *The Riddle of the New Testament*, London, Faber and Faber Limited, 1958, p. 9.

the American rock musician Elvis Presley: Gilbert B. Rodman, *Elvis*

after Elvis: the Posthumous Career of a Living Legend, London, Routledge, 1996.
Jesus' male ancestors: Matt. 1:1-16.
pregnant by the Holy Spirit: Matt. 1:18.

Chapter 2 Jesus and his heavenly Father

a voice from the sky: Mark 1:11.
the Spirit sent him away: Mark 1:12.
Matthew's elaboration of the story: Matt. 4:1-11.
a quotation from the ancient Jewish scriptures: Matt. 4:7, quoting OT Deuteronomy 6:16.
a unique knowledge of God: Matt. 11:26-27.
If you are Son of God: Matt. 4:3; 4:6.
impure spirits: Mark 3:11.
not to make him known: Mark 3:12.
he claims outright: Mark 14:62.
'Why do you call me good?': Mark 10:18.
the twelve-year-old Jesus: Luke 2:42.
as some modern scholars point out: *The New Jerusalem Bible*, London, Darton, Longman & Todd, 1985, p. 1691, note q.
he confers royalty upon them: Luke 22:29.
the only Son of God: John 1:14.
the Father loves the Son: John 5:20.
the Father has sent him: John 5:23, and in several other passages.
only the Son has seen the Father: John 6:46.
the Father glorifies him: John 8:54.
he knows the Father: John 8:55.
I and the Father are one: John 10:30.
deliberately undefined and hints at a more comprehensive and a profounder unity: *The New Jerusalem Bible*, p. 1769, note p.

is clearly meant to refer... to a unity in eternal being: John Marsh, *The Gospel of Saint John*, London, Penguin Books, 1968, p. 407.

what Joachim Kahl has identified as a structural principle of Christian theology: Joachim Kahl, *The Misery of Christianity: A Plea for a Humanity without God*, translated by N. D. Smith, Harmondsworth, Penguin Books Ltd, 1971, pp. 152-153.

Rudolf Bultmann declares: in *Jesus and the Word*, translated by Louise Pettibone Smith and Erminie Huntress Lantero, London, Collins fontana books, 1958, p. 17.

Chapter 3 Jesus and his earthly father

two brief references to Joseph: John 1:45 and 6:42.
According to Matthew: Matt. 1:18-19.

but did not sleep with Mary (so Matthew says) until the time when she gave birth to a son: Matt. 1:25.

Although this is at odds with the Orthodox and Roman Catholic dogma of Mary's perpetual virginity, the Greek text does seem to imply that Joseph did have intercourse with Mary after Jesus' birth. Some manuscripts even have 'until she gave birth to her first-born son', which really does suggest Joseph's part in the creation of other sons. This is how the translators of the *Authorized King James Version (1611)* understood the passage.

Joseph has another dream: Matt. 2:13-23, where still one more dream is reported.
'Isn't he the carpenter's son?': Matt. 13:55.
Plato talks about the maker and father of 'this everything': Plato, *Timaeus* 28c.
Luke mentions Joseph briefly: Luke 1:27; 2:4; 2:16; and again in 2:33.
a rather lame parenthesis: Luke 3:23.

story of the twelve-year-old Jesus: Luke 2:41-50.
the brief answer: 'Didn't you know that I must be busy with my Father's concerns?' This remark has been variously translated, but Whitland's translation here is closest to the Greek (and agrees, incidentally, with the *King James Version*: 'Wist ye not that I must be about my Father's business?').

brief, passing reference: Luke 4:22.
sweeping rejection of physical fatherhood in Matthew's Gospel: Matt. 23:9.

Chapter 4 Jesus and his mother

his family set out to take charge of him: Mark 3:21. The Greek words (*hoi par' autou*) that Whitland translates as 'his family' have been taken by some to mean 'his friends'. But it is certainly his family that turn up eventually at the house, and ask for him.
mentioned as the mother of Jesus: Mark 6:3. It is strange that Joseph is not mentioned here, although some Greek manuscripts do refer to Jesus as 'the carpenter's son.'
Mary was made pregnant by the Holy Spirit: Matt. 1:18.

Luke's version: Luke 1:26-27; 1:31.
since I do not know a man: Luke 1:34.
Adam knew Eve: OT Genesis 4:1.
The angel answered her: Luke 1:35.
the mother of my Lord: Luke 1:43.
the Magnificat: Luke 1:46ff.
Mary's first-born son: Luke 2:7.
Mary... ponders in her heart: Luke 2:19.
forty days after the birth: OT Leviticus 12:4; in the next verse the time

of blood purification for a female child is laid down as sixty-six days.

to present him... to the Lord: Luke 2:22-23.

hailed him as salvation: Luke 2:30-32.

this child is destined: Luke 2:34-35.

refers to Joseph... as 'your father': Luke 2:48.

one further indirect reference: Luke 11:27-28. The nursing mother Mary, whom Jesus does not acknowledge here, later became one of the main icons of the Catholic Middle Ages.

The first occasion is at Cana: John 2:1-12.

120 gallons of water into the best wine: the editors of *The New Jerusalem Bible* translate John 2:6 'six stone jars... each could hold twenty or thirty gallons.' This certainly implies hundreds of guests, which is not impossible in a closely-knit rural community in the eastern Mediterranean.

Jesus himself is the divine bridegroom: Mark 2:19-20; cf. Matt. 9:14-15; Luke 5:33-35.

addressing her curtly as 'woman' — *gunai*, in Greek: John 2:4. *The New Jerusalem Bible* comments (note c, p. 1747): 'Unusual address from son to mother; the term is used in John 19:26 [at the crucifixion], where its meaning becomes clear as an allusion to OT Genesis 3:15, 20; Mary is the new Eve, 'mother of the living.'

Sophocles' masterpiece, King Oedipus: line 726.

a Samaritan woman that he meets at a well: John 4:21.

the woman caught committing adultery: John 8:10 (where the woman is also addressed by Jesus as 'woman').

Mary's part in the drama: John 19:25-27.

the unusual term 'woman': *The New Jerusalem Bible*, note l p. 1787. But could a word as common as *gunai* (vocative of *gune*), which occurs nine times in the Gospels (usually in addressing a stranger) really

strike any ordinary reader of the Gospels as a reference to or echo of a specific text in the Old Testament?
a link with the verse in the Old Testament: Genesis 3:20.

as one modern writer has asserted: Erich Fromm, *The Dogma of Christ*, London, Routledge & Kegan Paul, 1963, p. 52.
Nativity with a capital N: the corresponding word is spelt with a capital N in French, Spanish and Italian, for example.

as Marina Warner remarks: Marina Warner, *Alone of All Her Sex: the myth and cult of the Virgin Mary*, London, Picador (Pan Books Ltd), 1985, p. 4.

Luke states quite clearly: Luke 1:27.

For some reason, however, the *New English Bible* translates the word *parthenos* as 'girl'. (It is sometimes maintained that the word is an echo of the Greek (Septuagint) OT Isaiah 7:14, where it translates the Hebrew word *almah*, which means simply a 'young woman'). It is true, as Professor Kamada remarks, that the notion that Mary was a virgin creates a problem for some present-day Christians. But even the angel Gabriel seems to have been a bit muddled on the question, because he calls David (the 10th-century BC King of Israel) the 'father' (i.e. ancestor) of Jesus (Luke 1:32).

a virgin for ever: the Council's deliberations were, of course, conducted in Greek, and Mary was declared *aeiparthenos*. The word has an interesting history. It was probably invented by the Greek poetess Sappho (7th century BC), who applies it to Artemis, the ancient Greek goddess of wildlife. The Jewish philosopher Philo, a contemporary of Jesus who wrote in Greek, says that the followers of Pythagoras applied the word to the number 7, because it was neither a factor nor a multiple of any number up to 10. Philo also calls the Jewish Sabbath *aeiparthenos* (Philo 1.46).

a verse in Matthew's Gospel: Matt. 1:25. *The King James Version* accepts, also, the manuscript reading 'first-born son'.

the references to Jesus' brothers and sisters: Mark 3:31-35; 6:2-6; Matt. 12:46-50;13:53-58; Luke 8:19-21.

the words 'brothers' and 'sisters'... can also mean 'half-brother', 'cousin' or 'near relative': see *The New Jerusalem Bible*, note o, p. 1631, on Matt. 12:46: 'not necessarily Mary's children but possibly near relations, cousins perhaps, which both Hebrew and Aramaic style "brothers", see OT Gen.13:8, 14:16, 29:15 ' (and other OT references). **Pope John Paul II has declared that Jesus was Mary's only child, and that she was a virgin both before and after his birth:** as reported in *The Times*, London, 30 August 1996.

in John's Gospel, where Jesus claims that he existed before Abraham: John 8:58. In an article on 'eternity' in the *Collier Macmillan Encyclopaedia of Philosophy*, New York, London, 1967, Vol. 3, pp. 63-66, Whitland's late philosophy tutor, William C. Kneale, states that the notion of timeless life passed into Christian theology from Plato's *Timaeus*. 'As early as the St John Gospel', Kneale writes, 'there is a curious passage in which Jesus is represented as saying, "Before Abraham was I am." But it is fairly clear that the author of this Gospel knew something of Greek philosophy, possibly at second hand through the works of the Jewish theologian Philo of Alexandria, and also that his narrative is no mere historical record of the life of Jesus.'

the dispenser of grace: Fromm, op.cit., p. 53.

not dogmatically defined: see Timothy Ware [now Father Kallistos Ware], *The Orthodox Church*, London, Penguin Books, 1963, p. 262.

prayers are addressed to Mary: one evening prayer in the Greek Orthodox holy prayer-book addresses Mary as 'spotless, incorruptible, immaculate, chaste Virgin, bride of God', and so forth, before whom the person praying declares himself to be a vile sinner in thought, word and deed, who offers a prayer from filthy lips, and so on (*Hiera Synopsis*, [*Apodeipnon*]), Athens, N. Alikiotis & Sons, 1952, pp. 74-76.

A survey of 2,011 French citizens conducted by the Institut CSA in 1998 showed that while 67 per cent of them never prayed at all, of the 33 per cent who prayed either daily, regularly or occasionally, the majority prayed to the Virgin Mary, rather than to Jesus Christ (reported in the Paris daily *Le Monde*, 22 May 1998).

Chapter 5 Jesus' brothers and sisters

another passage in Mark: Mark 6:2-6.
brother of... Judas: the Judas mentioned here is not, of course, Judas Iscariot. Matthew 13:53-58 reports the same incident, calling Joset 'Joseph', and referring to 'all his sisters' which suggests that there were at least three or four of them.

five different women named Mary: Marina Warner in her book *Alone of All her Sex: the myth and cult of the Virgin Mary*, London, Weidenfeld and Nicolson, 1976, meticulously lists the relevant passages in 'Appendix B: A Muddle of Marys', pp. 348-349.

the miraculous catch of 153 fish: John 21:11. A. N. Wilson, *Jesus*, London, Flamingo, HarperCollins Publishers, 1993, p. 61, suggests the number is symbolic of the number of converts to Christianity that had been made by that time. He refers to J. A. Emerton, 'The Hundred and Fifty-Three Fishes in John XXI:11', *Journal of Theological Studies*, April 1958, pp. 86-89.
woman in Bethany: Mark 14:3-9.
the mother of Zebedee's sons: Matt. 20:20; 27:56.

Chapter 6 Jesus against the blood family

the Greek words *oikos* and *oikia*: at Luke 12:52 and Luke 18:29.
Matt. 10:36 has *hoi oikiakoi*, 'those in the same house; the household'.
nowhere to rest his head: Matt. 8:20.
In the story in Mark's Gospel: Mark 3:35.

the family in its usual modern sense: when churchmen and politicians
talk about 'family values', they are invariably referring to the physical,
not the spiritual family. A striking example was furnished by a letter to
The Times (London) from the Bishop of Hull (11 January, 1997), taking its cue from what the bishop called 'your excellent leading article
on politics and the family'. He went on to ask 'which political parties
are going... to include in their manifesto specific proposals to change
the tax and benefits system in favour of families.' This is to identify the
family quite explicitly as, for example, French tax law does, with the
physical, economic (i.e. taxable) unit gathered round a hearth (the
foyer fiscal).

Most politicians, of whichever party, pay lip service to 'family values', which they often link to 'the Judaeo-Christian tradition'. Tony
Blair has no exclusive right among members of Parliament to invoke
this tradition. So, for example, John Redwood, whose wife, Gail, is also
quoted in an interview with Nigel Farndale in the *Sunday Telegraph
Magazine*, London,9 February 1997: 'John — and Gail — Redwood
are anything but embarrassed about their own enthusiasm for
Christian family values'.

most extreme passage: Luke 14:26.

One modern translator: J. B. Phillips, *The New Testament in Modern
English*, London, Geoffrey Bles, 1960.
much as English expounders of the New Testament love... inverted

commas: they are, for example, sprayed all over the pages of N. T. Wright's book *The New Testament and the People of God*, London, SPCK, 1992.

Another modern translation: *The New Jerusalem Bible*, note d, p. 1715.

with an eye on intelligent Gentile readers: Graham N. Stanton, *The Gospels and Jesus*, Oxford University Press, 1989, p. 82. The word 'intelligent' here is Professor Stanton's. But on the other hand, Luke 10:21 reports Jesus thanking his heavenly Father for concealing 'these things [i.e. the gospel] from wise and intelligent people'. This saying is also reported by Matthew (11:25), and is assumed to come from the source (known by scholars as 'Q') used by them, but not by Mark. For a claim to reconstruct Q (from the German word *Quelle*, 'source') in its entirety, see Burton L. Mack, *The Lost Gospel: The Book of Q and Christian Origins*, Shaftesbury, Dorset, Element Books Limited, 1993. The verse in Luke 10:21 and Matt. 11:25 is quoted on p. 89.

a noticeably watered-down form: Matt. 10:37.
This notion is presented elsewhere in Matthew's Gospel in another form: Matt. 19:29. Not all the Greek manuscripts include 'wife' in the list. 'For my sake' is my translation of the Greek words 'for the sake of my name' — the word for 'name' (*onoma*) can mean 'person' in *koine* Greek. Luke 18:29-30 has a similar saying to Matthew, but in Mark's version, Jesus, in what may be an ironical aside, promises those who desert their families for his sake persecution as well as tangible rewards in this world and eternal life in the age to come. Luke and Matthew have apparently edited Mark by cutting the remark about persecution.
Let the dead bury the dead: Matt. 8:22; Luke 9:60.
a dusty answer: Luke 9:62.

Rivalry between church and synagogue: John Macquarrie, *Jesus Christ in Modern Thought*, London, SCM Press, 1990, p. 90.

Brother will betray brother: Mark 13:12.

But Luke... leaves it out: Luke 21:16. Matthew has the prediction that children will put their parents to death, but puts it in a different context: Matt. 10:21.

another of Jesus' outbursts: Luke 12:51-53.

an echo of Micah: OT Micah 7:6. Matthew, who does not have Luke's motive, gives a version of the same prophecy that is even closer to Micah. He adds, 'and a man's enemies will be his own household' — words that come straight out of Micah (Matt. 10:36; Micah 7:6). So perhaps we have the true words of Jesus here.

Chapter 7 Jesus rules out divorce

most uncompromising in Mark's Gospel: Mark 10:2-9. The questioners were in fact Pharisees.

male and female: OT Genesis 1:27. In both Mark 10:6 and Matt. 19:4, the editor of the Oxford (Clarendon Press) Greek text of the Gospels for some reason prints the word for male (*Arsen*) with a capital letter, and that for female (*thelu*) with a lower case letter. But this distinction is not to be found in other Greek texts of the Gospels, for example that printed for United Bible Societies by the Württenberg Bible Society in Stuttgart, or in the verse in Genesis in Whitland's copy of the Septuagint (Greek version of the Old Testament) published in Athens in 1950 by the Adelphotes Theologon e Zoe; and it is either a slip in the Oxford text or an example of sexist bias.

Later in the same chapter: Mark 10:10-12. The word 'marries' here also may imply simply 'sleeps with'.

after divorcing her husband: scholars do not agree on the question whether or not Jewish women could divorce their husbands in first-century Palestine. At any rate, it seems unlikely that women of low social rank were able to do so. Ben Witherington III, *Women in the Ministry of Jesus*, pp. 26-27 has a detailed discussion of this point.

two almost identical passages: Matt. 5:32 and Matt. 19:9.
To some Roman Catholic scholars: a full explanation of the possible meanings of *porneia* here is given in *The New Jerusalem Bible*, note b, p. 1641 on Matt. 19.9.
spelt out at length in the Old Testament: OT Leviticus 18:2-18.

one passage in Matthew: Matt. 15:19. Here Jesus lists the things that make a person unclean, but lists of this kind are more in Paul's style than in Jesus' (Paul, Letter to the Galatians, 5:19-21; Letter to the Romans, 1:29-30).
in both versions of the Ten Commandments: OT Exodus 20:1-17; Deuteronomy 5:6-21.
Biblical scholars seem to agree: see, for example, W. R. F. Browning, *A Dictionary of the Bible*, Oxford University Press, 1996, p. 7; Ben Witherington III, *Women in the Ministry of Jesus*, Cambridge University Press, 1984, p. 20.

one of his most famous sayings: Matt. 5:28. It is not one, however, that is easy to translate. The words Whitland has translated as 'with desire' are usually translated 'with lust' or 'lustfully', but although the Greek word refers to physical desire, it neither has nor ever has had (according to Whitland) any especially reprehensible connotations (these are due, he thinks, to northern Puritanism). Ben Witherington III, in the book just quoted, tries to make the woman the desiring person (but why in that case is the adultery committed in his heart?), and he makes this absurdly anachronistic comment: 'This saying is at one and the same time a reaffirmation of man's leadership and responsibility for the community welfare, and an attempt to liberate women from a social stereotype.' Apart from doing violence to the Greek,

Witherington's interpretation brings in modern terms such as 'welfare' and 'social stereotype' which are, to say the least, far remote from the conceptual scheme of the Gospels.

the woman caught in the very act of adultery: in some Greek manuscripts of John, Chapter 8 (see below).
honour your father and your mother: Mark 7:10; Matt. 15:4.
the curt answer: Matt. 8:22; Luke 9:60.

Chapter 8 Jesus rescues a woman from stoning

some Greek manuscripts of John's Gospel: where it is placed between chapters 7 and 8.
his authorship has to be ruled out: the detailed argument against John's authorship is given in John Marsh, *The Gospel of St John*, London, Penguin Books, 1991, p. 682.
the author may have been Luke: see, for example, *The New Jerusalem Bible*, note u, p. 1761.
But Jesus bent down and began to write: this is the only mention in the Gospels of Jesus (or anyone else) writing as an action witnessed at the time. Elsewhere in the Gospels, the verb 'to write' is almost invariably in the passive voice, and refers to what has been written in the Hebrew scriptures.

John Marsh: pp. 683-684. According to Marsh, this passage 'puts into narrative form the theological truth that the Son did not come into the world to condemn it, but to deliver it.' Marsh also comments that the incident is placed in the Temple, 'the place where Judaism is thought to be preserved in its purity.' He links the incident with Jesus' assertion in John 8:15: 'I judge no one'.

The ancient Jewish law prescribing penalties for adultery: OT Deuteronomy 22:22.

Chapter 9 Jesus and the Kingdom of God

the Old Testament prophet Daniel: OT Daniel 2:44-45; 7:27.
his remarkable book: E. P. Sanders, *The Historical Figure of Jesus*, London, Penguin Books, 1993 pp. 171-175.
his royal status is not from this world: John 18:36. These words are usually translated 'my kingdom is not of this world', but the Greek says 'from this world', and the Greek word *basileia* can mean 'royalty' (as in Luke 22:29).
eating and drinking in the Kingdom of God: Luke 22:16-18; 22:30.
Rudolf Bultmann warns his readers: in *Jesus and the Word*, p. 35.
parable of the weeds that grow in wheat fields: Matt. 13:24-30.
Explaining the parable: Matt. 13:36-43.
the prince of this world: John 12:31.

Chapter 10 Jesus and the end of the world

Jesus explains the harvest: Matt. 13:39-40.
especially German theologians in the last two centuries: conspicuous among them are Johannes Weiss (1863-1914), Albert Schweitzer (1875-1965), Rudolf Bultmann (1884-1976), and Jürgen Moltmann (1926-).
According to Mark: Mark 13:5-37; compare Matthew 24 and Luke 21.
the more lurid ancient Jewish prophecies: for example, the books of Esdras (Ezra), which are included in some Bibles.
a modern author: E. P. Sanders, *The Historical Figure of Jesus*, p. 174.
one of the most extraordinary statements in the Gospels: Mark 13:30.

Hermann Reimarus: Reimarus (1694-1768) was a teacher of oriental languages in Hamburg. He did not begin writing until he was 60, and the work in question here, *The aims of Jesus and his disciples* (Vom Zwecke Jesu und seine Jünger: 42-44) was published posthumously. Reimarus was born in the same year as Voltaire, and could be described as a rationalist in the spirit of the (European) Enlightenment, but he was, like Voltaire, a deist. In the work quoted, he also stressed the Old Testament background to Jesus' beliefs, and portrayed him as a traditional Jew — a view that has been confirmed in a series of books by the Professor Emeritus of Jewish Studies at Oxford, Geza Vermes.

Chapter 11 Was Jesus insane?

A modern historian of the Jews: Salo Wittmayer Baron, *A Social and Religious History of the Jews*, 2nd ed., Vol II: *Ancient Times*, Part II, New York, Columbia University Press, 1952, p. 58.
Jesus' own family thought he was out of his mind: Mark 3:22.
too much for Matthew and Luke: Matt. 12:46-50; Luke 8:19-21.
raving mad: John 10:20.
possessed by a demon: John 8:48.

eternal damnation and torment: see pp. 85.
punishment... for other people's crimes: Jesus' promise to the lawyers and Pharisees: Matt. 23:33-36.
blessed are those who make peace: Matt. 5:9.
I have come not to bring peace, but a sabre: Matt. 10:34.
just as your heavenly father is perfect: Matt. 5:48.
his yoke is easy and his burden is light: Matt. 11:30.
only God is good: Mark 10:18.
sent by God to save the world, not to judge it: John 3:17. There is an

even more obvious contradiction at John 8:15, where Jesus says, 'I judge no one, but if I do judge, my judgement is true.' John Marsh tries to mitigate the dottiness of this remark by translating it, 'yet even if I do judge', but there is no 'yet even' in the original Greek.

in one chapter... and in another: John 5:31 and 8:14.

Belief alone can comprehend the paradox: William Hubben, *Dostoevsky, Kierkegaard, Nietzsche and Kafka*, New York, Touchstone (Simon & Schuster), 1997, p. 21.

Chapter 12 Threats and curses in the Gospels

many promises: Matt. 5:1ff.

abound in dire curses: for example, 'Woe to you rich! Woe to you who have plenty to eat! Woe to you who are laughing now — you will mourn and weep!' These words are put into Jesus' mouth in Luke 6:24-25.

threats of eternal fire: Mark 9:43.

being flung into the outer darkness: Matt. 22:13.

of wailing and gnashing of teeth: Matt. 8:12; 13:42; 13:50; 22:13; 24:51; 25:30.

of worms that never cease to gnaw: Mark 9:48.

of being cut to pieces: Matt. 24:51; cf. Luke 12:46.

of torture: see below, on Matt. 18:34.

the fate of slaves: Luke 12:47-48.

an enigmatic remark: Matt. 10:25.

Even in the Kingdom of God there is... a pecking order: it may reverse the order of this world, as in Luke 22:24-30, but Jesus tells his disciples on that occasion that they will eat and drink at his table in his kingdom, and sit on thrones to judge the twelve tribes of Israel. In a strange passage in Matthew (20:23), however, Jesus warns his disciples that he himself is not in charge of the seating arrangements in his kingdom. Matthew 19:28 repeats the promise of the twelve thrones (it must be presumed that someone not present takes over Judas Iscariot's throne), and Matthew 19:30 reports the saying, often misquoted, that (in the Kingdom of Heaven) 'many of the first will be last, and the last first' — again indicating a hierarchy, even if it largely reverses the earthly rank order.

the punishments for unfaithful and negligent church officials are stark: Robert J. Karris O.F.M. in *The New Jerome Biblical Commentary*, London, Geoffrey Chapman, 1992, p. 705.

Jesus' promise to the lawyers and synagogue Jews: Matt. 23:33-36. The same threat is reported in Luke 11:49-51, who words the final remark: 'Yes, I tell you, an answer will be sought from this generation.'

In the course of cursing these Jews seven times: Matt. 23:13-36.

the slaying of Abel: OT Genesis 4:8. Abel's murder is the first death to be reported in the Bible.

Zechariah was actually stoned to death: OT 2 Chronicles 24:21. His murder is the last one to be described in the Old Testament.

the erudite Dr G. B. Caird: G. B. Caird, *The Gospel of St Luke*, London, Penguin Books, 1990, p. 159.

no ethical idealism, but an urgent moral realism: Sir Edwyn Hoskyns and Noel Davey, *The Riddle of the New Testament*, London, Faber and Faber Limited, 1958, p. 139.

According to a recent newspaper report: *The Sunday Telegraph*, London, 16 March 1997.

a jealous God attributing the sins of the fathers to their children: OT Exodus 20:5.

the Greek dramatist Euripides: *ta ton tekonton sphalmat' eis tous ekgonous hoi theoi trepousi* — 'the gods turn the faults of the parents to the offspring', a fragment quoted by the 19th-century Italian scholar I. G. Orelli, commenting on Horace's *Ode* III.6.1, which threatens the Romans with punishment for the faults of their ancestors.

Freud claimed that religious beliefs were not derived from experience: Sigmund Freud, *The Future of an Illusion*, Vol. XXI, Standard edition, p. 17.

the German-American psychologist Erich Fromm: in *The Dogma of Christ and Other Essays on Religion, Psychology and Culture*, London, Routledge & Kegan Paul, 1963, pp. 19ff.

torturers: Matt. 18:34. This is the ordinary sense of the Greek word here, and most translators accept it, although Liddell & Scott have 'gaoler' (but only in this instance). The word does not occur elsewhere in the New Testament, although related words meaning 'torture' or 'torment' do occur.

those chosen: Matt. 22:14, where Jesus explains another parable about the Kingdom of Heaven with the remark that many are invited, but few are chosen.

worst horrors... reserved for the life to come: some people in this life are also described as being in torment (Matt. 4:24; 8:6, for example).

in agony in these flames: Luke 16:24.

a Church of England 'working party': reported in *The Times*, London, 15 July 1996, p. 5, 'Synod backs rethink on traditional view of Hell' by Ruth Gledhill, Religion Correspondent.

In January 1996, the Doctrine Commission of the Church of England published a report, *The Mystery of Salvation*, asserting that Hell is a state of annihilation ('total non-being') rather than eternal torment: *The Daily Telegraph*, London, 11 January 1996.

According to Luke: Luke 12:5.

according to the prophet Isaiah: OT Isaiah 30:33.

another threat of hellfire: Matt. 5:22.
more references to Gehenna: Matt. 5:29-30.
Another collection of fierce threats of hellfire: Mark 9:43-49.

Fire features in other threats: false prophets are compared with a tree that does not produce good fruit: it is cut down and thrown into the fire (Matt. 7:19). 'I have come to bring fire to the earth' Jesus tells his disciples (Luke 12:49) — obviously symbolic fire say the editors of *The New Jerusalem Bible* in a note on this verse, although not everyone has interpreted it that way.

In one parable: Matt. 22:1-14.
a learned commentator explains: *The New Jerusalem Bible*, p. 1645, note a.

Chapter 13 Power fantasies

several references to... the authority with which he preaches: for example, Mark 1:27; Matt. 7:29; Luke 4:32.
the authority to forgive sins: Mark 2:10; Matt. 9:6.
authority to exorcise impure spirits: Matt. 10:1.
a word that can sometimes be translated as 'miracle': Mark 6:2; 9:39. Cf. also Matt. 11.20; 13:58.
the Messiah coming in the clouds with great power: Mark 13:26.
according to Matthew's account: the authenticity of the Gospel accounts of Jesus' trial have been challenged by a number of modern scholars, notably by Paul Winter in his book *On the Trial of Jesus* Berlin, Walter de Gruyter & Co, 1961. Dr Winter settled in England in 1947, after having joined the free Czech Army and fought in North Africa and Europe. He pursued his researches in libraries at Oxford during the day, while earning a bleak livelihood as a night watchman at a home for epileptics and as a railway porter, but at last had the sat-

isfaction of seeing his vastly erudite book received with the acclaim it deserved (see his obituary in *The Times*, London, 28 October 1969).

sitting on the right hand of power: Matt. 26:64.

reported in Matthew and Luke: Matt. 4:5-7; Luke 4:9-12.

a very high mountain: Matt. 4:8.

a possible 'height complex'... in Nietzsche: this is explored in an essay by F. D. Luke in 'Nietzsche and the Imagery of Height' in *Nietzsche: Imagery & Thought*, edited by Malcolm Pasley, London, Methuen, 1978, pp. 104-122.

sexual temptation or arousal: Luke 7:36-50, for example.

forty years... forty days: the number 40 had symbolic significance in the ancient Middle East. In a monograph of enormous erudition, *Die Tessarakontadenlehren der Griechen und anderen Völker*, Köln. Sächs Gesellschaft Berichte B61, 1909, W. H. Roscher traced the significance of the number 40 back to ancient Babylon, where the number 7 was held in awe because of the seven stars visible to the naked eye in the Pleiades cluster, and special importance was attributed to the seven 40-day periods in human pregnancy.

innermost thoughts: OT Deuteronomy 8:2.

a striking phrase: Aline Rousselle, *Porneia: on Desire and the Body in Antiquity*, translated by Felicia Pheasant, Oxford: Basil Blackwell, 1988, p. 142.

only one conflict for him: Rousselle, p. 143.

debauched her in his heart (Matt. 5:28): according to an ancient idea, the heart was the location of thoughts and fantasies. In the passage from Deuteronomy referred to above, the innermost thoughts are located in the heart. To this day, one can hear a Greek say that 'God sees the heart' (cf. OT 1 Samuel 16:7); and the word kardiognostes 'knower of hearts', first used of God in NT Acts 1:24, is quite com-

monly applied today to a person who seems to be naturally endowed
with psychological insight.

Chapter 14
Sexual misdemeanours before Noah

a passage in Matthew's Gospel: Matt. 24:37-39; cf. Luke 17:26-27.
eating and drinking and...: Matt. 24:38; Luke 17:27.
according to the Old Testament Book of Genesis: OT Genesis 6:4-8.
indulging all the time in evil fantasies: OT Genesis 6:5.
God decided to wipe the whole lot out: OT Genesis 6:13.
seven mating couples of some specially selected creatures: OT Genesis
7:2.
**They could eat animals only if they chewed the cud and had divided
hooves:** OT Leviticus 11:3-8.
God, who liked the smell of burnt meat: OT Genesis 8:21.
Noah... got drunk and behaved badly: OT Genesis 9:20-21.

Luke uses the passive form: Luke 17:27, *egamizonto*.
a strange and difficult passage in one of St Paul's letters: 1 Corinthians
7:36-38.

from the time of Homer to the present day: Liddell & Scott cite Homer,
Odyssey I 36, saying that the word refers to 'mere sexual intercourse'.
They also cite later authors using the word in this sense.

Chapter 15 Did Jesus have a partner?

as Susan Haskins... remarks: in her book *Mary Magdalen: Myth and Metaphor*, London, HarperCollins Publishers, 1993, p. 82.
Jesus was about thirty: Luke 3:23. Some scholars have taken John 8:57 to imply that Jesus was in his forties.

an authoritative writer: Peter Brown, *The Body and Society: Men, Women and Sexual Renunciation in Early Christianity*, London, Faber and Faber, 1989, p. 41.
Pliny briefly describes such a community: *Natural History*, V.15.73: *gens sola et in toto orbe praeter ceteras mira, sine ulla femina, omni venere abdicata, sine pecunia, socia palmarum.*
still used to mean 'mistress': it is probably a translation of the Greek word *hetaera*, meaning 'courtesan'. For the Greek element in southern Italian dialects, see G. Rohlfs, 'Das Griechentum Unteritaliens', in his book *An den Quellen der romanischen Sprachen*, Halle (Saale), 1952, pp. 108-124, and other books and articles by the same author.

a complex drama: see Elaine Pagels, *The Gnostic Gospels*, London, Penguin Books, 1985, pp. 13-32.
earlier discoveries in Egypt: at Behnesa in Upper Egypt. These manuscripts are known, from the ancient name of Behnesa, as the Oxyrrhynchus Papyri (papers made from the stem pith of an aquatic plant). They were discovered in their thousands in the 1890s by two British scholars, B. P. Grenfell and A. S. Hunt, and included a collection of fourteen sayings of Jesus.
a theological treatise, not remotely comparable in form with the New Testament gospels: Graham N. Stanton, *The Gospels and Jesus*, Oxford University Press, 1989, p. 131.
the most important among the women who followed Jesus in his ministry: Mary Magdalene's claim to this title is convincingly argued by

Carla Ricci in her book *Mary Magdalene and many others: Women who followed Jesus*, translated from the Italian by Paul Burns, Tunbridge Wells, Burns & Oates, 1994.
a leading scholar: R. McL. Wilson, *The Gospel of Philip, Translated from the Coptic text, with an Introduction and Commentary*, London, A. R. Mowbray & Co, 1962, p. 35.

partners in crime: Matt. 23:30 ('partners in the blood of the prophets').
partners in a fishing business: Luke 5:10.
a bricklayer's mate: Plato, *Republic*, 333b (written about 380 BC).
his pupil Aristotle: *Nicomachean Ethics*, 1133b (undated, but probably written about 340 BC).
a man in love is useless: Plato, *Phaedrus* 239c.
dialogue on love: Plato, *Symposium*, 208e-209c, where the argument is attributed to Diotima, a priestess from Mantinea in Arcadia, who is supposed to have instructed Socrates on love.
illicit sexual intercourse: Plato, *Laws*, 784e. The word *koinonia* also means sexual intercourse in some classical Greek playwrights.

the homosexual male habit of cruising: Plutarch, *Erotikos* (*The Dialogue on Love*), 750b.
paederasty involves sexual partnership: *The Dialogue on Love*, 752a.
no woman ever produced a child without the partnership of a man: Plutarch, *Advice to Bride and Groom*, 145d.

And the consort of Christ: R. McL. Wilson, *The Gospel of Philip*, p.36.

one scholar takes 'the others' to mean the other women in Jesus' entourage: Dr W. C. Till (quoted Wilson p. 115).
a... book about them by an Italian scholar: Carla Ricci, *Mary Magdalene and many others: Women who followed Jesus* — see above.

about the Gnostics: see, for example, Elaine Pagels, *The Gnostic Gospels*, London, Penguin Books, 1985; Hans Jonas, *The Gnostic Religion*, Boston, 1958; R. McL. Wilson, *The Gnostic Problem*, London, 1958; Giovanni Filoramo, *A History of Gnosticism*, translated by Anthony Alcock, Oxford, Basil Blackwell, 1990.

Even in... the Lord's Prayer: Matt. 6:9-13. Luke's version, however, does not lend itself to the same dualistic interpretation (Luke 11:2-4). In Matt. 11:25, too, Jesus addresses God as 'Father, Lord of heaven and earth' (cf. Luke 10:21).

John's Gospel in particular was influenced by Gnosticism: in John's Gospel, there are three references to the 'ruler of this world' (12:31; 14:30 and 16:11) that are squarely in the dualistic tradition that in the Middle Ages gave rise to the heretical Christian sects of the Bogomils and the Cathars.

a sect founded by a poet and philosopher: see R. McL. Wilson, *The Gospel of Philip* and the same author's *Valentinus and Valentinianism*, *The Encyclopaedia of Philosophy*, London, Collier Macmillan, 1972, Vol.8, pp. 226-227.

just as probable as his turning 120 gallons of water into wine, or feeding four or five thousand people with five loaves and two fishes: John 2:1-11 (water into wine); Mark 6:35-44; Matt. 14:15-21 — 5,000 men (not counting women and children) fed with five loaves and two fish; Mark 8:1-9 ; Matt. 15:32-38 — 4,000 men (not counting women and children) fed with seven loaves and a few fish.

Chapter 16 Was Jesus homosexual?

In a newspaper interview: The *Sunday Telegraph*, London, 30 June 1996: 'Preparing himself for a party in Heaven: Me and My God: Hugh Montefiore talks to Frances Welch'. Bishop Montefiore has described his 'simple and momentous' conversion, when he was sitting in his school study one afternoon, and 'indulging in an adolescent muse' in his book *On Being a Jewish Christian: its Blessings and its Problems*, London, Hodder & Stoughton, 1998, pp. 13-14.

Carla Ricci has explored this silence: *Mary Magdalene and Many Others: Women who followed Jesus*, Tunbridge Wells, Burns & Oates, 1994. Chapter 2, 'A text the exegetes forgot' on Luke 8:1-3, is particularly interesting.

one passage in John's Gospel: 13:23.
another chapter in John's Gospel: John 19:26.
the one who reclined at the supper on Jesus' breast': John 21:20.

a modern theologian: Anders Nygren in his book *Agape and Eros* makes this point several times, e.g., p.110, p. 210.

Feelings of such universal love are, however, claimed by some Christians: in a letter to the editor of *The Times*, London, on 19 February, 1997, the Rev. Canon John Halliburton wrote of 'the few of us in the Anglican tradition who for many years now have been involved in the ecumenical movement, and knowing and loving both Europe (Eastern and Western) and the Third World, remain profoundly concerned that Christians should work together.' The distinction here between Eastern and Western Europe is interesting, because in Christian sectarian terms the north-south divide is more significant, in the case of Germany, even within one country: see Arthur Schopenhauer, 'On Religion', in *Parerga and Paralipomena*, translated by E. F. J. Payne, Oxford, Clarendon Press, 1974, Vol.2, p. 329.

the kiss that Judas gave: Mark 14:45.
asserted or implied by some writers: Hyam Maccoby, *Judas Iscariot and the Myth of Jewish Evil*, London, Peter Halban, 1992, p. 138, and note 16, p. 186.

the eroticism of the relationship between Jesus and Judas: Hyam Maccoby, *Judas Iscariot* , p. 138. This part of his book is based, perhaps largely, on an article by Sidney Tarachov, 'Judas the Beloved Executioner', in *Psychoanalytic Quarterly* (New York), 29, 1960, pp. 528-554.

killing as love or in the service of love: Sidney Tarachov in the article just referred to, p. 534.

the well-known Japanese custom: Tarachov, p. 535. Tarachov, whose method of argument is discursive rather than rigorous, goes on to say: 'In the cases of the willing victim there is a remarkable similarity to the Christ myth', and among other parallels he says that Judas is the analogue of the friend who finishes off the person who commits harakiri by decapitating him.

in the Greek of Matthew's Gospel, *Hetaire*: Matt. 26:50.

a member of one's gang — a crony: see the fragment (usually attributed to Archilochus) discovered by R. Reitzenstein in 1899 in the University Library at Strasbourg (discussed in Eduard Fraenkel, *Horace*, Oxford, at the Clarendon Press, 1957, pp. 27 ff). In his book, Fraenkel translates the line containing the word *hetairos* as 'he who was once on our side'. In his lectures on Horace, however, he referred to 'a member of our gang'.

The word *hetairos* **occurs in only two other places in the Gospels, both in Matthew, and in parables in each case:** 20:13 (a landowner addressing one of his hired labourers); and 22:12 (where a king so addresses one of his subjects, one casually invited off the street to a wedding reception).

The word *hetairos* was occasionally used in classical Greek to mean 'lover', and the feminine form of the word, *hetaira*, meant 'companion' or 'courtesan' (cf. the English word 'hetaera'). Several derivatives of the basic word in ancient Greek had sexual connotations — words meaning, for example, 'meretricious', 'harlotry', 'a lewd man', and 'a female homosexual'. (Liddell & Scott s.v. *hetaira*).

a crony, in fact. That is not the same as friend: the German scholar A. Schlatter, however, gives a number of examples from Josephus of the use of the word *hetairos* to stress a strong relationship of friendship (in *Der Evangelist Matthäus*, Stuttgart, Calwer, 1957, p. 590, quoted in William Klassen, *Judas: Betrayer or Friend of Jesus*, London, SCM Press Ltd, 1996, p. 113, note 35). William Klassen also writes (p. 103): 'Whereas the term [*hetairos*] was used by Matthew in a context of a subordinate who was in the wrong, "it has a deeply profound meaning that the master who spoke a word of woe towards the betrayer (Matt. 26:24), in the moment of betrayal addresses him with the name of a trusted member of the inner circle," a *chaber*'. Klassen is here quoting another German source, namely E. Lohmeyer and W. Schmauch, *Das Evangelium des Matthäus*, Göttingen, Vandenhoeck & Ruprecht, 1958, p. 364.

the same word that Luke uses: Luke 7:38, 45.
recent studies of Judas' role: see Hyam Maccoby's book, and the references there. He singles out the article by Sidney Tarachov mentioned above.

the man you love is ill: John 11:3.
looked at him in the face and loved him: Mark 10:21.
except that the love indicated was stronger than a mere liking: but Matthew and Luke, although probably basing their version of this incident on Mark, do not explicitly mention Jesus' love for the young man: Matt. 19:16-22; Luke 18:18-23.

at the end of John's Gospel: John 21:15-17. There is no word 'all' in the Greek text, in spite of the *New English Bible's* version of 21:15.
three times: Carla Ricci, in the book already quoted, pp. 127-128, comments on the significance of the number three in the Gospels, and more generally in the Greek and Hellenistic-Roman worlds, and quotes the German scholar G. Delling's article on 'three' in the *Theologisches*

Wörterbuch zum Neuen Testament 8 (1969), pp. 215-222, to the effect that in the New Testament 'three sometimes has the value of a precise number', and 'when certain actions or certain facts appear three times, this means that they are complete, finished, definitive'.

denied that he knew Jesus: Mark 14:66-72; Matt. 26:69-75; Luke 22:54-61; John 18:16-18 and 25-27.

the Greek verbs used by the Gospel writers: various forms of *agapao* and *phileo*.

when used by pagan Greek writers: the fourth-century BC writer of comedies Anaxilas uses the word *agapao* to mean making love to a courtesan, and Aristotle (4th century BC) and Lucian (2nd century AD) use the verb (but rarely) in the sexual sense.

Chapter 17 The love that dare not speak its name

the agony in the garden: Mark 14:32-42; Matt. 26:36-46.
deeply sad, to the point of death: Mark 14:34; Matt. 26:38.

Susan Haskins' remark: in *Mary Magdalen: Myth and Metaphor,* London, HarperCollins Publishers, 1993, p. 82.

a man who looks at a woman with desire: Matt. 5:28.
the terrifying advice to tear your own right eye out: Matt. 5:29. Cf. Matt. 18:9; Mark 9:47.
those who have castrated themselves for the sake of the kingdom: Matt. 19:11-12.
no marriages there: Mark 12:18-27; Matt. 22:23-33; Luke 20:27-40.
quoting ancient biblical authority: OT Genesis 1:27; 2:23.
Jesus recognizes this bond only between male and female: Mark 10:6; Matt. 19:4.

The Gospels repeat: Mark 12:30; Matt. 22:37; Luke 10:27.
the Old Testament command: OT Deuteronomy 6:4-5.
to love your neighbour as yourself: OT Leviticus 19:18; Mark 12:31;
Matt. 22:39; Luke 10:27.
on a mountain in Matthew's Gospel: Matt. 5:1.
to love their enemies: Matt. 5:44; Luke 6:27.

Freud... raised this particular difficulty: in *Civilization and its Discontents*, Vol. 21, standard edition, pp. 109-110.

a love that does not discriminate seems to lose some of its own value: it may be significant that the Latin word for 'to love' occurring in key verses of the version of the Gospels that was for centuries the only one used by the Roman Catholic Church (the Vulgate) is *diligere*, a weaker word than the more common amare. By etymology, *diligere* (from *dislegere*) means 'to choose, to single out'. This is the word used in the Vulgate at Mark 10:21 — *Jesus autem intuitus eum, dilexit eum* — Jesus looked at him and loved him.

the Greeks have a word for that: the word *storge*.
is derived from what he calls 'genital love': others, of course, had maintained this before Freud. The French philosopher Denis Diderot (1713-1784) once told one of the contributors to his *Encyclopedia* that there was 'a bit of testicle at the bottom of our most sublime sentiments and most refined tenderness'. (Quoted in Peter Gay, *The Enlightenment: The Science of Freedom*, New York, W. W. Norton & Company, 1977, pp. 189-190).
Plato's guests at his drinks party: Plato, *Symposium* 178a (Phaedrus) and 195a (Agathon).
comparatively late on the Greek scene: he is not one of Homer's gods, but makes his first bow in the *Theogony* of Hesiod, who is later, though not much later, than Homer (probably 8th century BC).

Eros is not a god, but a great demon: Plato, Symposium, 202d.

the charcoal-burner worried by law-suits: see M. S. Silk and J. P. Stern, *Nietzsche on Tragedy*, Cambridge University Press, 1981, p. 162. These two authors say that the Greek religious outlook 'was not, and could not have been, the invention of the common man or an invention on his behalf. It is too sophisticated, but, above all, it is too *aristocratic*.' (Emphasis in the original.)

very little is known about his religious beliefs or feelings: E. R. Dodds has a chapter, 'The Religion of the Ordinary Man in Classical Greece', in his book *The Ancient Concept of Progress*, Oxford, Clarendon Press, 1973, pp. 140-155. He remarks (p. 141) that 'the inner side of Greek religion escapes us; we can study it only in its external, collective aspect, as a social phenomenon. And even about the beliefs implied in collective acts, it is hard to speak with any confidence.' Professor Dodds confirms M. S. Silk's view when he says that traditional Greek religious beliefs were those of a fighting aristocracy (p. 143).

Chapter 18 Sexual love and death

a trick question to Jesus: Mark 12:18ff; also Matt. 22:23-33; Luke 20:27-40.
the snide question to Jesus: Mark 12:23.
how Luke reports Jesus' words: Luke 20:34-36.

A learned modern commentator: G. B. Caird, *The Gospel of St Luke*, London, Penguin Books, 1990, p. 224.

that future state: so, at Luke 18:30, 'the coming age' (where there is life eternal) is contrasted with 'this time'. The Greek word for 'age' is *aion* (from which, English 'aeon') and the word for 'eternal', *aionios*, derives from it.

those judged worthy: Luke 20:35. This is one of very few explicit references to any possible human merit in the Gospels.

a pleasingly ironic comment by the Scottish philosopher David Hume: in his *Natural History of Religion*, Works, IV, 315, n, where he refers to 'the importance and dignity of the province of copulation'. For the early Christian theologian Origen, however, apparently 'no amount of decorum in the sexual act could smooth away the incongruities associated with it': Peter Brown, *The Body and Society: Men, Women and Sexual Renunciation in Early Christianity*, London, Faber and Faber, 1989, p. 174.

linked to a verbal form used... to emphasise repeated or habitual actions: the verb in question has an *-isk-* affix that had this force in an ancient Greek dialect, once spoken on what is now the Mediterranean coast of Turkey. The ancient Greek tribal dialects had more or less faded out by New Testament times, but there is no doubt that a few dialect features survived in the common Greek of the eastern Mediterranean (and indeed survive to this day). That this may have happened to the *-isk-* verbs is made more likely by the fact that some still survive in Cypriot Greek, and Cyprus is the nearest Greek island to Palestine (see Mondry Beaudouin, *Étude du Dialecte Chypriote*, Paris, Ernest Thorin, 1884, pp. 94-95).

The common Greek of Jesus' day was in many respects nearer to modern Greek than to the ancient Greek local dialects that it superseded. Now in modern Greek, the verb *gamo* (a contracted form of the ancient Greek *gameo*) means only one thing, 'to fuck' (although, unlike the English word, it is almost always used in its literal sense, and relatively seldom in an abusive sense or as an expletive). This modern usage perhaps does tend to confirm the suggestion that in this chapter of St Mark's Gospel, it is not simply wedding bells that are being ruled out in the world of the risen dead. In ancient Greek, too, although the verb and its derivatives usually mean 'to marry', it is used occasionally, as the Liddell & Scott lexicon puts it 'of mere sexual intercourse', in Homer, for example, and Euripides.

expressed himself in more moderate language: in the Greek of Jesus' day, however, one cannot say whether the word *gameo* used of 'mere sexual intercourse' would have sounded moderate or immoderate.

the link that, according to Luke, he makes: Luke 20:35-36.

fervent upholder of the virtue of sexual asceticism: so Marina Warner, in *Alone of All her Sex: the myth and cult of the Virgin Mary*, London, Weidenfeld and Nicolson Ltd, 1976, p. 33.
Adam and Eve's disobedience, as reported in the Old Testament: OT Genesis 3:1-6.
where there is death, there too is sexual coupling: St John Chrysostom, *De Virginitate*, quoted in Julia O'Faolain and Lauro Martines, eds. *Not in God's Image*, London 1973, p. 138 (see Marina Warner, *Alone of All her Sex*, p. 52).
When Eve was in Adam, there was no death: R. McL. Wilson, *The Gospel of Philip*, Translated from the Coptic text, with an Introduction and Commentary, London, A. R. Mowbray & Co, 1962, p. 44. Wilson comments on this saying of Philip's, 'Death... is not as for Paul the wages of sin, but the result of the separation of the sexes.' (The reference to Paul is to the Letter to the Romans 6:23.)

imperatives of sexual reproduction that condemn us to dusty death: see, for example, Roger Gosden, *Cheating Time: Science, Sex and Ageing*, London, Macmillan, 1996.

Freud wrote about 'an instinct of death or destruction': see *Civilization and its Discontents*, (Vol.21, standard edition) and *Beyond the Pleasure Principle*, 1920.
a fragment of the ancient Greek dramatist Sophocles: Fragment 953 (A. C. Pearson, editor, Cambridge, 1917): *thanonti keinoi sunthanein eros m'echei.*

For Ryuji the kiss was death: *The Sailor Who Fell from Grace with the Sea*, translated from the Japanese by John Nathan, London, Penguin Books in association with Martin Secker & Warburg Ltd, 1970, pp. 62-63.
hara-kiri as a supreme sexual act... a double suicide for love: see Henry Scott Stokes, *The Life and Death of Yukio Mishima*, London, Peter Owen, 1975, pp. 245-249.

their Freudian significance: the Freudian significance of the reference to dagger and sheath (*Romeo and Juliet*, Act V, Scene III) would have been obvious to the dimmest of Shakespeare's groundlings.
supreme bliss: the *Liebestod* in *Tristan and Isolde* ends with the words *höchste Lust.*

Chapter 19 Jesus recommends self-castration

a far more fierce saying: Matt. 19:11-12.
except in one particular case: see p. 56.

not everyone can accept: the Greek could also be translated, perhaps 'not everyone can put his head round what I am going to say.'

what I am going to say: the Greek says 'this saying', and Liddell and Scott cite passages showing that 'this' in Greek can refer to what follows. Whitland's translation links, as the word translated 'accept' also does, the first sentence in Jesus' remark with the last: 'Let anyone accept this who can.' Other translations, however, take the words 'this saying' to refer back to verses 8-9 (the remark about divorce).

the ninth century king of Israel, Jehu: OT 2 Kings 9:30-37. Jehu made such a thorough job of the trampling, that only Jezebel's skull, feet and hands could be found afterwards. Jehu attributed this to God, who had, he believed, promised the prophet Elisha that dogs would eat Jezebel, so that no one could bury her (1 Kings 9:10).
a fifth-century prophet: he was a follower of the second Isaiah, but his words are incorporated in the OT book of Isaiah, 56:3-5.

a prim footnote: *The New Jerusalem Bible*, p. 1641, note c.
the word 'castrated': Matt. 19:12, *eunouchisthesan*.

the first Christian to be a genuinely philosophical theologian: Origen (185-253 AD) is so described by Robert M. Grant, 'Origen', in *The Encyclopaedia of Philosophy* (Paul Edwards, Editor in Chief), London, Collier Macmillan Publishers, 1967, Vol.5, p. 551.
human sexuality and other seemingly indestructible attributes of the person: Peter Brown, *The Body and Society: Men, Women and Sexual Renunciation in Early Christianity*, London, Faber and Faber, 1989, p. 167.
always a limit and a source of frustration: Peter Brown, *The Body and Society*, p. 164.

the story related by Eusebius: in his *History of the Church*, Book VI.
a modern scholar has doubted his story: H. E. Chadwick, *Early Christian Thought and the Classical Tradition*, Oxford University Press, 1966, p. 67.
quite a common practice: details will be found in Aline Rousselle,

Porneia: On Desire and the Body in Antiquity, translated by Felicia Pheasant, Oxford, Blackwell, 1988, pp. 121-128. Mlle Rousselle deals with pagans rather than Christians, and she is at pains to establish that the fact that some men deliberately removed their testicles 'did not mean that they renounced desire or sexual activity'.

the very matter-of-fact manner: Peter Brown, *The Body and Society*, p. xviii.

the Roman priest Hippolytus: in chapter 16 of his *Apostolic Tradition*, quoted by Aline Rousselle in *Porneia*, p. 103. In a footnote Mlle Rousselle notes the categories of persons, taken over from Roman civil law, that the early Christians refused to baptise, which included gladiators, charioteers, male and female prostitutes, and pimps. To these the Christians added, among others, sculptors, painters, magicians, jugglers, and teachers. A full list is to be found in Erich Fromm, *The Dogma of Christ*, London, Routledge & Kegan Paul, 1963, pp. 39-40, note 1.

a fourth-century collection of regulations: these are known as the *Apostolic Canons*. There are 85 canons, probably compiled by a Syrian monk, and presented as a supplement to the so-called apostolic constitutions. Canons 22 and 24 are those quoted here.

Old Testament authority: OT Deuteronomy 23:1.

The sixth-century Persian empire: according to the Greek writer, Xenophon, in his historical novel, *The Education of Cyrus*, Book VII, chapter 5, the king Cyrus the Great first recruited eunuchs because he thought they would be more loyal than other men. Cyrus' belief that eunuchs were just as ambitious as other courtiers was proved right by Byzantine history.

the Greek historian Herodotus: *Herodotus* VII.104 ff. This is actually the first historical (as distinct from fictional) mention of eunuchs in Persian history, and it refers to the reign of Xerxes (485-465 BC).

chaste abstinence: the Rev. Thomas Sheldon Green's entry in his *Greek-English Lexicon to the New Testament*, London, Samuel Bagster and Sons, 1972, for the word *eunouchizo*.
as one modern commentator: William Neil's *One Volume Bible Commentary*, London, Hodder and Stoughton, 1973, p. 344.

the sacred scriptures have various levels of meaning: Origen, *De Principiis*, Book IV.
dashed the severed portions of themselves against the image of the cruel goddess: Sir James Frazer, *The Golden Bough*, 1890, p. 581.
dressing in women's clothes: *Varro Mem.* CXX describes them as sexy (*venusta*).

whose worship Jezebel had introduced into Israel: OT 1 Kings 16:31 (through her husband, Ahab, king of Israel).

Latin poets: Lucretius, *On the Nature of Things*, 2.600-643; Catullus, *Carmina*, 63 ('Attis'). There is a fine verse translation of Lucretius by Sir Ronald Melville (Oxford, Clarendon Press, 1997, with introduction and explanatory notes by Don and Peta Fowler). James Michie has translated Catullus for modern readers (London, Rupert Hart-Davis, 1969, with introduction and notes by Robert Rowland).
spurious woman: *notha mulier.*
Hippolytus in his massive *Refutation of All Heresies*: Book V, Ch.17.
Another opponent of heresy, Tertullian: *Apology*, Ch.15.

Chapter 20 Jesus and women's rights

one contemporary authority: Ben Witherington III, *Women in the Ministry of Jesus: a Study of Jesus' Attitudes to Women and their Roles as Reflected in His Earthly Life*, Cambridge University Press, 1984, p. 10.

his account of God... in exclusively masculine terms: see, for example, Matt. 11:27.

accompanied on his travels by a number of women: Luke 8:3.

Carla Ricci's book on this subject: *Mary Magdalene and many others: Women who followed Jesus*, translated from the Italian by Paul Burns, Tunbridge Wells, Burns & Oates, 1994. The silence of the commentaries is the subject of an entire chapter, 'A Text the Exegetes forgot'.

bishops, priests and deacons: these words derive, respectively, from the Greek *episkopos, presbuteros,* and *diakonos.*

not even in Jesus' vocabulary: although the words *presbuteros* and *diakonos* do occur in the Gospels, they are not used in the sense they acquired as the Christian hierarchy evolved.

one female deacon: Phoebe, in Paul's Letter to the Romans, 16:1.

all God's beloved people in Rome: Letter to the Romans 1:7.

some of his followers would be servants there: see, for example, Matt. 20:27. Jesus goes on to say that he himself came 'not to be served, but to serve'.

Jesus did not make any obvious distinction: Susan Haskins, *Mary Magdalen: Myth and Metaphor*, London: HarperCollins Publishers, 1993, p. 13, remarks: 'Nowhere in the texts is there any indication that Christ regarded the women's contribution as inferior or subsidiary to that of his male disciples'.

the head of every man is Christ: 1 Corinthians 11:3.

an American humorist: James Thurber (1894-1961).

Chapter 21 Mary Magdalene

according to Luke's Gospel: Luke 8:1-3.

We know very little: Susan Haskins, *Mary Magdalen: Myth and Metaphor*, London, HarperCollins Publishers, 1993, p. 3.

a beautiful woman with long golden hair: Haskins, p. 3.

the prototype of the penitent whore: Marina Warner, *Alone of All Her Sex: The myth and cult of the Virgin Mary*, London, Weidenfeld and Nicolson, 1976, p. 232.

first mention: Luke 8:2.
She is identified by her place of birth: Haskins, p. 14 comments: 'of the women described [in Luke 8], Mary Magdalene alone stands out undefined by a designation attaching her to some male as wife, mother or daughter; and she is the only one to be identified by her place of birth. It is therefore as an independent woman that she is presented; this implies that she must also have been of some means, to have been able to choose to follow and support Christ.' Haskins also notes that Mary Magdalene's birthplace was 'el Mejdel, a prosperous fishing village on the north-west bank of the lake of Galilee, four miles north of Tiberias. It was destroyed in AD 75 because of the licentious behaviour of its people'.

listed among the women present at the crucifixion of Jesus: Mark 15:40; Matt. 27:56; John 19:25.
a witness, indeed... the witness: Haskins, p. 4.
Mark states expressly: Mark 15:46-47.
he continues his account: Mark 16:1-8.
another Salome: Mark 6:21-29; Matt. 14:3-12.

Matthew's and Luke's versions of events: Matt. 28:1-10; Luke 24:1-12.
a unique role: John 20:1-18.
Marks states... that the sun had risen: Mark 16:2. But some manuscripts say the sun was still rising (the difference is between an aorist participle and a present participle of the verb).
men, as Luke recounts, in shining clothes: Luke 24:4.
the other disciple the one Jesus loved: John 20:2.
he saw and he believed: John 20:8.

The Gospel continues: John 20:11-18.

Rabbouni: according to Haskins (following John Marsh, *The Gospel of St John*, London, Penguin Books, 1985, p. 63), a word usually reserved for God (although other commentators interpret the word differently: see Haskins, note 16, p. 404).

Do not cling to me: the famous *me mou aptou* on which Haskins p. 10 comments: 'Mary Magdalene is to infer [from Jesus' remark that he has not yet gone up to the Father] that her relationship with Jesus has now changed, that any kind of physical contact which she might have had with him formerly is no longer appropriate.'

every interpretation that has accumulated around her: Haskins, p. 11.
unlike the eleven male disciples: Haskins, p. 13.

Chapter 22 Salome, the dancing princess

according to Mark: Mark 6:22-23.
Mark made this bit up: it is not in Matthew's account of the same incident. Matthew simply says that Herod promised on oath to give her anything she asked for.
an Old Testament story: OT Esther 5:3; 5:6.

the Gospels do not say: Mark 6:14-28; Matt. 14:3-12.
Herod was afraid of the mob: Matt. 14:5.
Mark continues the story: Mark 6:25-28.

an element of folklore: this is probably an understatement. No less an authority than Rudolf Bultmann calls Mark's account of John the Baptist's death 'entirely legendary', *Jesus and the Word*, p. 27.

Flaubert is said to have drawn inspiration from a sculpture: according to the French critic Maurice Nadeau, in *Gustave Flaubert Ecrivain*, Paris, Editions Denoël, 1969.

petite princesse: the title that Flaubert conferred on her. She came from Damascus, and described herself in Turkish as *küçük hanim* (which is more like *petite madame*) because at that time (1850), Egypt was still nominally part of the Ottoman (Turkish) Empire, although governed by the Albanian warlord Mehemet Ali. Flaubert's descriptions of *küçük hanim's* dances can be read in *Flaubert in Egypt*, translated and edited by Francis Steegmuller, London, Penguin Books, 1996, pp. 113-118.

Salome, who is known to history from other sources: Josephus, *Antiquities of the Jews*, 18.5.

the Salome who was a follower of Jesus: Mark 15:40.

among the women who visited Jesus' empty tomb: Mark 16:1-8.

Chapter 23 Jesus and the street-walker

the episode of the woman who gatecrashed the Pharisee's dinner party: Luke 7:36-50. Carla Ricci, *Mary Magdalene and many others: Women who followed Jesus*, p. 91, comments on this episode: 'Luke brings out the woman's personality in all its complexity: mannerisms, means of expression, ways of relating and communicating, sensibilities and feelings, tears and upset, need for touch and tenderness.'

Salo Wittmayer Baron: in his *A Social and Religious History of the Jews*, 2nd ed., Vol. II: *Ancient Times*, Part II, New York, Columbia University Press, 1952, p. 38.

a group that Jesus cursed seven times: Matt. 23:13-38.

whitewashed tombs: (Matt. 23:27) this is *The New Jerusalem Bible's* translation of the expression that the *Authorized King James Version* renders as 'whited sepulchres'.

the parable of the Pharisee and the tax collector: Luke 18:9-14.
wife-swappers: Luke 18:11. In view of the ancient Jewish definition of adultery, this translation may come nearer in atmosphere to the original than the more conventional one does.

a sign of her fallen status: Susan Haskins, *Mary Magdalen*, p. 18.

this guy: the Greek (v. 39) simply says 'this one', but this was a distinctly derogatory way of referring to someone, and Whitland's translation is intended to convey this.
not one descriptive adjective or adverb in the whole passage: sometimes the sense is reinforced by the use of a compound verb, such as the verb translated above as 'covered with kisses' (a sense brought out in *The New Jerusalem Bible* and J. B. Phillips' translation, but missed in the *New English Bible*).

Chapter 24 Jesus and prostitutes

this limited and prejudicial list of women's roles: Ben Witherington III, *Women in the Ministry of Jesus: a Study of Jesus' Attitudes to Women and their Roles as Reflected in his Earthly Life*, Cambridge University Press, 1984, p. 11.

where the word occurs (in the plural) in Luke: Luke 15:30.
a curious detail which seems to have attracted very little comment: Jonathan Kirsch, however, notes that Matthew 'identifies four women from the Hebrew Bible as Jesus' direct ancestresses: Tamar, Rahab, Ruth, and Bathsheba. Notably, all four of these women are non-

Israelites who married Israelite men, and all four engaged in sexually questionable conduct, including prostitution and seduction' — Jonathan Kirsch, *The Harlot by the Side of the Road: Forbidden Tales of the Bible*, New York, Ballantine Books, 1997, p. 142.

Matthew traces Jesus' lineage: Matt. 1:1-17.

described as a common prostitute: a *zonah* in Hebrew in OT Joshua 2:1.

The story of Rahab: OT Joshua 2:1-21; 6:22-25.

her faith: Paul, Letter to the Hebrews, 11:31.

justified by her deeds: Letter of James, 2:25.

the Jews were... forbidden to allow the practice of sacred prostitution: OT Deuteronomy 23:18 (the Hebrew word here is *qedeshah*).

famous parable of the prodigal son: Luke 15:11-32.

complains bitterly to his father: Luke 15:29-30.

his famous reply: Luke 15:32.

he refers sympathetically to them: Matt. 21:31-32 (see below).

Jesus tells the chief priests and Jewish elders in the Temple: Matthew 21:32.

Jesus himself was accused: Mark 2:16 (some manuscripts omit the words 'and drinking').

Look, a glutton and a wine drinker, a friend of tax collectors and sinners: Matt. 11:19.

tax collectors and prostitutes go into the Kingdom of God ahead of you: Matt. 21:31-32. Luke makes the same point in a different context, but though he mentions the tax-collectors, he keeps quiet about the prostitutes (Luke 7:29).

E. P. Saunders (*The historical figure of Jesus*, London, Penguin Books, 1993, p. 234) comments 'God intended to include even the wicked in the kingdom. Jesus did not want the wicked to remain wicked in the interim, but he did not devise a programme that would enable tax collectors and prostitutes to make a living in less dubious ways.'

a passing mention by a public speaker: *Aeschines* 1.119.
the second-century satirist Lucian: Lucian, *Menippus*, 11.

Chapter 25 The woman with expensive perfume

another story... in the other three Gospels: Mark 14:3-9; Matt. 26:6-13; John 12:1-8. They agree in setting it a few days before the crucifixion. Matthew's version of it is the same as Mark's, with one or two minor differences in the wording, and it is generally assumed that Matthew's source for the story was simply Mark. John's version, however, is materially different from Mark's on a number of points.

Both Mark and John place the incident in Bethany, a village (which still exists) near Jerusalem: but while Mark puts it in the house of a leper named Simon, John seems (though he does not say so in as many words) to have it take place in the house of the two sisters Mary and Martha.

Simon is introduced as a Pharisee: Luke 7:37.
in Mark and Matthew, he is called a leper: Mark 14:3; Matt. 26:6.
In only one other place: Mark 10:29.

the plot thickens: John 12:1-9.
John attributes a sinister motive to Judas: John 12:6.
so that she 'may keep the ointment for the day of my burial': John 12:7.
Mary of Bethany's prophetic role: Susan Haskins, *Mary Magdalen*, p. 24.

a general trend... to blacken the Jews: in his book, *A Jewish Understanding of the New Testament*, New York, University Publishers

Inc., 1956, p. 269, Dr Samuel Sandmel points out that in John's Gospel, 'the opponents of Jesus are no longer the Pharisees and Sadducees and the chief priests and the council, but simply "the Jews."...Jesus is portrayed as though not a Jew.'

In John's Gospel there are 67 references to 'the Jews', compared with five in Matthew, seven in Mark, and five in Luke.

a most fateful development for the history of anti-Semitism: Hyam Maccoby, *Judas Iscariot and the myth of Jewish Evil*, London, Peter Halban, 1992, p. 63.

Chapter 26 Mary and Martha

the only women... that Jesus is said to have loved: John 11:5. The verse reads: 'And Jesus loved Martha and her sister and Lazarus.' Susan Haskins, *Mary Magdalen*, p. 21, comments: 'John's strange emphasis has been seen to imply that the relationship between the sisters and Christ was closer than that between Christ and Lazarus, or that they were somehow more important in the eyes of the evangelist.'

one of the sisters poured ointment over Jesus' feet: in the Lazarus story, John identifies Mary (11:2) by referring to this episode, which he describes at length in 12:1-8.

Lord, the man you love is ill: John 11:3.

that the son of God may be glorified: John 11:4. The meaning of these words is not immediately apparent, but Jesus may be hinting that the miracle will bring about his death, which will also bring him glory.

the Father who has sent me: John 6:44; 8:18, and other references in John.

meeting of the official leaders: John 11:47-53.

John also says: John 12:10-11.

The poor man Lazarus... in Luke's Gospel: Luke 16:20-25.

some learned commentators: see, for example, Ronald Brownrigg, *Who's Who in the New Testament*, London, J. M. Dent, 1993, p. 147.

Mary and Martha... in Luke's Gospel: Luke 10:38-42.
what is this one thing: The various Greek manuscripts have slight variations in their version of this incident. Some of the Church Fathers quote 'a few things are needed', or 'a few things are needed, or one thing'. The editors of the *The New Jerusalem Bible* accept this reading, and comment: 'In his remark, Jesus rises from the material plane ("few things are needed", i.e. for the meal) to the "one thing necessary", which is to listen to the word of God' (p. 1707, note j).

But this seems to weaken the point Jesus made (although as expressed here, the opposition between 'many' and 'one' is a characteristically Greek rather than an ancient Hebrew or Aramaic notion).

One modern translator: J. B. Phillips, *The New Testament in Modern English*, London, Geoffrey Bles, 1960.
apart from Mary Magdalene: John 20:16.

Chapter 27 The woman at the well

the Samaritans were not only foreigners: on the Samaritans, see Salo Wittmayer Baron, *A Social and Religious History of the Jews*, 2nd ed., Vol. II: Ancient Times, Part II, New York, Columbia University Press, 1952, pp. 26-35.

Samaria was the region of ancient Palestine lying between Galilee to the north and Judaea to the south. The majority of its inhabitants were descended from the ancient Israelites and could trace their origins back at least a thousand years to the time of the first kings of Israel, and they observed the rules laid down in the first five books of the Old Testament. But they began to break away from the main body of the Jews towards the end of the sixth century BC, after the return from the exile to Babylon. By the end of the fourth century, if not before, they had succeeded in building a temple of their own on Mount Gerizim, a rival to the Jerusalem temple.

John Marsh, in *The Gospel of St John*, London, Penguin Books, 1991, p. 207, states that the Samaritans 'claimed, like the Jews, to be true descendants of Jacob, who gave Israel its name. Israelites would not consider them to be Jews, but the Samaritans claimed all the status and all the privileges of the Jews, disputing with them in many matters, theological and ecclesiastical.' He adds that suspicion and hostility marked the relationship between Samaritans and Jews.

amazed to find Jesus talking with a woman: John 4:27.
highly undesirable for a religious teacher to talk with a woman: John Marsh, p. 221. Carla Ricci in *Mary Magdalene and many others*, Tunbridge Wells, Burns & Oates, 1994, p. 65, quotes a Rabbinic treatise to the effect that a Rabbi should not have much conversation with his own wife, let alone with the wives of other men.

Even those comments, however, understate the shock to the disciples. According to D. Daube, *Journal of Biblical Literature*, LXIX (1950), pp. 137-147 (quoted by Marsh, p. 210), in Jewish law all Samaritan women were regarded as 'menstruants from their cradle'. For a Jew to drink from a common vessel with any one of them was to incur pollution.

As John tells the story: it is only in John (4:7-42).
God's gift: (v. 10) scholars have interpreted these words in several ways, but the most immediate way is to take them is as referring to Jesus himself.
living water... a spring of water leaping to eternal life: (verses 10 and 14) water has a high charge of symbolism in the New Testament, signifying life and spirit, purification and initiation.

and you Jews: (v. 20) this is the meaning, because the woman slips from addressing Jesus in the singular to the plural. Similarly, Jesus slips from addressing the woman in the singular ('Believe me, woman') to 'you [in the plural, i.e. you Samaritans] worship what you do not know' in verse 22.

a coded reference to the God of the Samaritans: Marsh, p. 215.
the theologian's urge towards maximum content: see page 25.
woman's five husbands represent the five foreign gods: Marsh, p. 215.
Another theologian: Ben Witherington III, *Women in the Ministry of Jesus*, p. 59. The emphasis in the text on the word simultaneously is Witherington's own.
the Old Testament book: OT 2 Kings 17:30-31. The foreign gods listed are Succoth-Benoth, Nergal, Ashima, Nibhaz, Tartak, Adrammelech and Anammelech.

Believe me, woman: (v. 21) see the note on John 2:4 in Chapter 4, where Jesus addresses his mother as 'woman'.

Chapter 28 Was Jesus a racist?

salvation comes from the Jews: John 4:22.

to conquer the proud: *debellare superbos*. The phrase is Virgil's (70-21 BC), *Aeneid*, 6. 853; but in the same line he does tell the Romans to remember to spare the humbled.

a warrior hero, who would destroy his enemies and restore Israel's sovereignty over the world: Rudolf Bultmann, *Primitive Christianity in its Contemporary Setting*, translated by Reginald H. Fuller, London, Collins The Fontana Library, 1960, p. 96.

all the kingdoms of the world and their glory: Matt. 4:8.

the Roman practice: the first emperor, Augustus, had to die before he was officially made a god, but the poet Horace, writing in 23 BC, says that while the sound of thunder makes him believe that Jove rules in heaven, here on earth 'Augustus will be held to be a god, now that the people of Britain and the glum Persians have been added to the empire' (Horace, *Odes* 3.5.1-4). But the emperor Claudius was worshipped at Colchester during his life.

a Greek, a Syrophoenician by race: Mark 7:26. The Greek word for 'race' here is the root of the English words 'genetic' and 'genocide'. Matthew describes the same woman as a Canaanite (Matt. 15:22).
sent only to the lost sheep of the House of Israel: Matt. 15:24.

do not head for any Gentiles: Matt. 10:5.
   A leading modern commentator on the New Testament , Dr C. H. Dodd, explains that Jesus was just as aware as any of his contemporary Jewish teachers of the 'long tradition that Israel is the people over which God is rightfully king, in and through which his kingdom is to be realised': C. H. Dodd, *The Founder of Christianity*, London, Collins Fontana Books, 1973, pp. 94-95. Dr Dodd adds (p. 103) that the messianic idea as popularly held 'meant both the rule of the Messiah over Israel and also the domination of Israel over the nations'.
   Dr Dodd's explanation of Matt. 10:5 is supported by another contemporary authority, Prof. D. E. Nineham, who in his commentary on Mark's Gospel writes 'the power of Jesus is not a general, but a particular spiritual power, and one that is associated with the Jewish race. For it is the power of the Messiah, the agent of *Israel's* God for the establishment of *His* kingdom and, in the first instance at any rate, the salvation of *His* people.' See D. E. Nineham, *Saint Mark*, London, Penguin Books, 1963, p. 199 (emphasis in the original).

Another great Protestant New Testament scholar, Rudolf Bultmann, who held the chair in that subject at Marburg University in Germany from 1921 to 1951, explained that although Jesus expected the Kingdom of God to arrive in 'a tremendous eschatological drama', his expectations did not square entirely with popular Jewish hopes.

In the thought of Jesus, he writes, 'the national connotation of the Kingdom of God remains in the background', but this 'does not mean that he taught its universality. He took for granted, as did his contemporaries, that the Kingdom of God was to come for the benefit of the Jewish people. See Rudolf Bultmann, *Jesus and the Word*, London, Collins Fontana Books, 1958, p.38 (emphasis in the original).

Prof. Bultmann' refers to Matt. 19:28; Luke 22:29-30, and Matt. 10:23. He does not mention Jesus' remark to the Samaritan woman that salvation comes from the Jews, and he says in the introduction to Jesus and the Word, 'the Gospel of John cannot be taken into account at all as a source for the teaching of Jesus.'

a curiously snide reference to the 'Gentiles of the world': Luke 12:30; cf. Matt. 6:32.

Why do the nations rage: OT Psalms 2:1.

cure of the Syrophoenician woman's daughter: Mark 7:24-30; Matt. 15:21-28.
Let the children eat their fill first: Mark 7:27; cf. Matt. 15:26.
the pagan woman in reply: Nineham, *Saint Mark*, p. 199 claims: 'She thus recognises the divinely ordained division between God's people and the Gentiles.'
or even 'doggies': see Nineham, *Saint Mark*, p. 201, who rightly objects to this translation.
the editors of *The New Jerusalem Bible***:** note h, p. 1635, on Matt. 15:26.

lessen the insult: but these same editors, commenting on OT Deuteronomy 23:18-19, show how insulting the word ('an opprobrious term for a male prostitute') could be in other contexts.

the Samaritan leper he cured: Luke 17:11-19.
the woman at the well: John 4:5-42.
the Old Testament prophet Daniel: especially OT Daniel 12:2.
the only one of ten lepers to thank Jesus for curing him: Luke 17:15.
the parable of the lost sheep: Matt. 18:12-13; cf. Luke 15:4-7. Luke adds a further parable to make the same point: 'which woman with ten drachmas,' he asks his disciples, 'if she loses one of them, does not light a lamp and sweep the house clean, and search carefully until she finds it? And when she has found it, doesn't she call her friends and neighbours together, and tell them, "Come and celebrate with me, because I've found the drachma I'd lost!" In the same way, there is joy among God's angels when one sinner repents.' (Luke 15:8-10).

one of the most learned of modern commentators on the Gospels: C. H. Dodd, *The Founder of Christianity*, London, Collins 1971, p. 94.

Chapter 29 Jesus cures a woman with a haemorrhage

according to the Gospels: Mark 7:29; Matt. 15:28.
not the only miracle that Jesus performed at a distance: see Matt. 8:5-13 (the cure of the centurion's servant).
curing his disciple Simon's mother-in-law of a fever: Mark 1:29-31; Matt. 8:14-15; Luke 4:38-39.
the name... which means 'Rock': Mark 3:16; Matt. 16:18.
she evidently got going with the housework: all three Gospels say that she began to wait on him (Jesus) or them (Jesus and the two brothers Simon and Andrew). The Greek word, from a derivative of which the

English word 'deacon' is in turn derived, often means to serve, or to wait at table: cf. John 12:2, the supper in Bethany at which Martha served.

the cure of the woman with a haemorrhage: Mark 5:25-34; Matt. 9:20-22; Luke 8:43-48.

a continuous uterine haemorrhage: D. E. Nineham, *Saint Mark*, London, Penguin New Testament Commentaries, 1990, p. 157. Carla Ricci suggests tentatively that the disorder may have been psychosomatic, *Mary Magdalene and many others: Women who followed Jesus*, pp. 99-100.

one modern biblical scholar: Nineham, *Saint Mark*, p. 158.

Luke describes 'a whole crowd' trying to touch Jesus: Luke 6:19.

according to traditional Jewish belief: OT Leviticus 15:25-30.

Luke the only Gospel writer: Luke 13:10-17.

weekly foretaste: G. B. Caird, *Saint Luke*, London, Penguin New Testament Commentaries, p. 171.

Chapter 30 Mary Magdalene's seven demons

Carla Ricci has made... the dominant theme of her book: the book was originally published in Naples in 1991 by M. D'Auria Editore under the title *Maria di Magdala e le molte altre: Donne sul cammino di Gesù*, and has been translated from the Italian by Paul Burns under the title *Mary Magdalene and many others: Women who followed Jesus* (Tunbridge Wells, Burns & Oates, 1994).

Jesus journeyed... out of their own resources: Luke 8:1-3.

Joanna is mentioned again by Luke: Luke 24:10.

as one of the women who followed Jesus from Galilee: Luke 23:55.

who, as Carla Ricci points out, must have left her husband: Carla Ricci, *Mary Magdalene*, pp. 154-156.

Dr Ricci also makes (p. 69) the interesting suggestion that Luke may have had 'rewarding conversations' with Joanna, 'who could have been the source of the information about Herod provided by Luke in his work'.

Carla Ricci's argument that there is a conspiracy of silence about these women: but E. P. Sanders, *The Historical Figure of Jesus*, London, Penguin Books, 1993, p. 109 suggests another interpretation when he writes that 'it is possible that... Luke... is exaggerating the degree to which Jesus and his band were supported by women, including one of some rank' (Joanna). Sanders points out that in the NT Acts of the Apostles, also written by the author of Luke's Gospel, the writer 'liked to call attention to the prominent women who supported first Jesus and then his apostles' (see Acts 17:4).

many women in his entourage: Luke 8:3.
unheard of — for a rabbi, a teacher to have been accompanied... by women: see Ben Witherington III, *Women in the Ministry of Jesus*, p. 117, and notes 232 and 233, p. 195. Witherington argues, however, that Jesus was not a feminist, in the sense of 'rejecting a patriarchal framework outright. Such a person would have felt it necessary to include at least one woman among the Twelve.'
regarded by most people at the time as social outcasts: see Susan Haskins, *Mary Magdalen*, pp. 13-14.

The number seven had — and still has — special connotations: some scholars derive the significance of the number 7 in ancient Middle Eastern culture from the seven visible stars in the Pleiades cluster; others from the seven visible planets; and still others, from the four lunar phases of seven days each. See above, p. 249 on the number 40; and Carla Ricci, *Mary Magdalene*, p. 131 for some further references. Jesus himself seems to have regarded seven demons as especially

malignant carriers of disease: see Matt. 12:43-45; Luke 11:24-26.

all four Gospels: Mark 1:16-20; Matt. 4:18-22; Luke 5:1-11; John 1:35-42.

Chapter 31
The widow who would give a judge a black eye

men lived longer on average: it has been estimated, however, that only four men in every hundred survived their fiftieth birthday (in contrast to today's figure, in advanced industrial countries, of only four or five men in a hundred failing to survive that day. Nowadays, even in countries with comparatively low life expectancy, about 20 per cent of the population live beyond the age of 50: see World Health Organisation's *World Health Report*, 1998). The average life expectancy of women at the time that the Gospels were written would have been brought down by the relatively high number of deaths in childbirth.

three thousand widows and virgins: according to John Chrysostom, the fourth-century archbishop of Constantinople, quoted in Peter Brown, *The Body and Society*, p. 148.

their low status in the eyes of the law: according to Carla Ricci, *Mary Magdalene and many others*, p. 76, quoting various authorities, widows were juridically on the same level as slaves and children, and were exposed to judgements and abuses of power that often reduced them to penury. This was aggravated by the fact that they could not inherit from their husbands and had no legal defenders.
Jesus... issued a warning: Mark 12:38-40; cf. Luke 20:45-47. Matt. 23:6-7 has a similar condemnation of 'scribes and Pharisees', but without any mention of widows.

legal managers of rich widows' estates: J. Duncan M. Derret, '"Eating up the Houses of Widows": Jesus's Comments on Lawyers?' *Studies in the New Testament*, vol.11, Leiden, E. J. Brill, 1977, pp. 120 ff. (quoted in Witherington, p. 17).

a widow who kept pestering a judge: Luke 18:1-8.

described as a beggar... by Mark: Mark 12:42-43. Luke, telling the same story, uses a poetical word that could bear a blander translation: Luke 21:1-4.

a leading German authority: Rudolf Bultmann, *History of the Synoptic Tradition* (translated by John Marsh), Oxford, Blackwell, 1963, p. 17.

According to Luke: 2:36-38.

the male child who opened the womb: Luke 2:23.

all who were waiting for the ransoming [i.e. messianic deliverance] of Jerusalem: Luke 2:38.

There were Jews who were waiting for a warlike leader who would drive the Romans and their puppet kings out of Palestine. Again, some Jews identified this figure with the awaited Messiah (about whom there were many different and indeed conflicting ideas circulating among the Jews of the first century). But the ransoming or deliverance that Anna implicitly forecast was a spiritual liberation.

Chapter 32
Jesus brings a widow's dead son back to life

Luke's Gospel... tells how Jesus raised a widow's dead son to life: Luke 7:11-17.

twelve-year-old daughter of a synagogue leader: Mark 5:22-24; 38-42; Matt. 9:18-19; 23-25; Luke 8:41-42; 49-56.

Lazarus is the most famous: this miracle is reported only by John

(11:38-44).

Jesus... stated his own belief in the resurrection of the dead: Mark 12:25-27; Matt. 22:29-32; Luke 20:34-40.
what is saved is a spiritual body: Paul, 1 Corinthians 15:44.
Jesus claimed that the dead had been raised: Luke 7:22.
the saying about entering the Kingdom of God with only one foot or only one eye: Mark 9:43-47; Matt. 5:29-30.
Matthew's report on the natural calamities that accompanied Jesus' death on the cross: Matt. 27:51-53.
from a later passage in the New Testament: Paul's first letter to the Corinthians 15:12.

a Matthean *midrashic* **gloss in paratactic style:** Benedict T Viviano, O.P., in *The New Jerome Biblical Commentary*, p. 672.
passages in the Old Testament about the resurrection of saints: for example, OT Isaiah 26:19.

Matthew was inspired... by some lurid passages in the Old Testament: e.g. Isaiah 26:19; Daniel 12:2; and Ezekiel's famous vision of the valley of dry bones that came to life and stood on their feet like a vast assembly (OT Ezekiel 37:1-10).
the story of the prophet Elijah visiting the town of Zarephath, where he brought a widow's son back to life: OT 1 Kings 17:17-24.
Luke refers to this very visit: Luke 4:25-27.

Luke has not only invented some parts of his Gospel: see, for example, E. P. Sanders, *The Historical Figure of Jesus*, London, Penguin Books, 1993, p. 120, pp. 176-177, p. 256. An interesting comment on Luke's imaginative literary technique is to be found in *The New Jerusalem Bible*, p. 1695, note g (on Luke 4:16-30).
disservice to the truth by omission: this is implied by E. P. Sanders,

op.cit., p. 258.

Some Christians are required by their Church to believe in miracles: this was laid down by the third session of the First Vatican Council of 1870.

Creed of Saint Athanasius: set out in *The Book of Common Prayer,* immediately after The Order for Evening Prayer. Athanasius was a fourth-century patriarch of Alexandria who combatted the heretical doctrine that Jesus was not of one substance with God the Father.

as Dr George Caird puts it: G. B. Caird, *Saint Luke*, London, Penguin Books, 1963, p. 109.

resurrection faith rests on the experiences of the disciples: Graham N. Stanton, *The Gospels and Jesus*, Oxford University Press, 1989, p. 270.

something happened to the followers of Jesus: E. P. Sanders, 'But did it happen?' in the *Spectator*, London, The Spectator (1828) Ltd, 6 April 1996, p. 17.

the occasional resurrection — even of a number of corpses simultaneously: Prof. Kamada is apparently referring to the rising of the saints in St Matthew's Gospel (Matt. 27:51-53).

Professor Hans Küng seems to say something similar: Hans Küng, *Credo: The Apostles' Creed Explained for Today*, translated by John Bowden, London, SCM Press Ltd, 1993, p. 109.

'resurrection' does not mean a return to life in this space and time: Hans Küng, p. 111.

As reported in the *Sunday Telegraph*, London, on 12 April 1998, Church of England bishops hold 'widely divergent views on the physical reality of the Resurrection [of Jesus]'. More than one bishop expressed the view that it would not have been possible to make a film of the event, while others stressed that the official teaching of the [Anglican] Church is that Jesus was raised bodily from the tomb. In an article in *The Sunday Times*, on 15 April 2001, the Bishop of St Albans, the Right Reverend Christopher Herbert, answered 'an unqualified yes' to the question whether he believed in the physical resurrection of Christ.

a slice of baked fish, which he took and ate in front of them: Luke 24:42-43. John 21:9-14 has a more elaborate version of this event, according to which Jesus invites his disciples to breakfast, and gives them bread and fish. But John does not actually say that Jesus also ate.

Chapter 33 Jesus in the Garden of Nature

neither nature alone nor art alone: so Gogol describes Plyushkin's garden in *Dead Souls*: 'In a word, all was as beautiful as neither nature nor art can contrive, beautiful as it only is when these two come together, with nature giving the final touch of her chisel to the work of man.' (Nabokov's translation in Nikolai Gogol, *Vladimir Nabokov*, New York, New Directions Books, 1961, p. 88).
an ancient view: eloquently put by Cicero (106-43 BC), *De Natura Deorum*, II. xxxii.
the beauty of the flowers of the field: Matt. 6:29; Luke 12:27.
a self-moved condition or system: *Diogenes Laertius* (third century, our era) vii. 148: *esti de phusis hexis hautes kinoumene*. The reference here is to the Stoics, but earlier Greek philosophers also held this view of nature, perhaps impicitly rather than explicitly. See R. G. Collingwood, *The Idea of Nature*, Oxford, Clarendon Press, 1945, p.82.

'sign' or 'portent' or 'wonders' or 'act of power': in Hebrew, *'oth, mopheth, niphla'oth* and *geburah*. In Greek, *semeion, teras, thaumasia* and *dunamis*.

the Greek word for 'nature' does not occur in the Gospels: it does, however, occur in Paul's letters (e.g. 1 Corinthians 11:14).

According to R. G. Collingwood, Aristotle distinguishes seven meanings of the word *phusis*: *The Idea of Nature*, pp. 80-82.. Plato uses the word in a concrete sense, equivalent to 'the creation' (*Protagoras* 315c; *Phaedo* 96a).

Jesus' native language — Aramaic — had no word corresponding to this Greek word: see M. Pohlenz, *Die Stoa*, Göttingen, 1948, I 401, quoted in Robert M. Grant, *Miracle and Natural Law in Graeco-Roman and Early Christian Thought*, Amsterdam, North-Holland Publishing Company, 1952, p. 269.

he once asked... whether grapes could be picked from thorns or figs from thistles: Matt. 7:16. There is a similar saying in Luke 6:44 — 'figs are not gathered from thorns, nor do they pick grapes from a bramble bush.'
the fig tree in leaf as a sign that summer is near: Mark 13:28-29; cf. Matt. 24:32-33; Luke 21:29-32.
the wind blows where it wants to: John 3.8. The irregularity of the movement of the wind in the sense of not obeying the laws of nature is, of course, only apparent. As David Hume remarked in 1748 (since when we have learnt all about isobars), 'the winds, rain, clouds, and other variations of the weather are supposed to be governed by steady principles; though not easily discoverable by human sagacity and enquiry': *An Enquiry concerning Human Understanding*, Sect. viii, Part 1, 68.

A. N. Wilson comments on the strange behaviour of the sower: A. N. Wilson, *Jesus*, London, Sinclair-Stevenson Limited, 1992, pp. 122-123, and the references to other writers there.
misunderstandings derived from legal text books: Wilson cites the incorrect description of the mustard shrub in the Talmud, and supposes that it may have been the source for Jesus' description of mus-

tard as the biggest of all herbs (Mark 4:30-32; cf. Matt. 13:31-32; Luke 13:18-19. Luke refers to it as a tree).

the fig tree that Jesus cursed: Mark 11:12-14; 20-25. Matt. 21:18-22 tells the same story in a slightly abbreviated form.
the only destructive miracle in the Gospels: Graham N. Stanton, *The Gospels and Jesus*, Oxford University Press, 1989, p. 214. (Prof. Stanton puts the word 'destructive' in inverted commas).
the two thousand pigs that Jesus caused to... drown in the Sea of Galilee: Mark 5:11-13; Matt. 8:30-32; Luke 8:32-33. Only Mark records the number of pigs.

Jesus meant to perform a symbolic action: *The New Jerusalem Bible*, on Matt. 21:19 (p. 1645, note d). The Old Testament reference is to Jeremiah Chapter 24, where *Yahweh* (God) compares the exiles in Babylon with good figs, but King Zedekiah and his men as bad figs who will be cursed and destroyed.
an elaboration of a parable recorded by Luke: Luke 13:6-9. See. Stanton, *The Gospels and Jesus*, pp. 214-215.

they made no effort to understand the world of nature: see Robert M. Grant, *Miracle and Natural Law in Graeco-Roman and early Christian thought*, p. 93. Prof. Grant also observes that the word 'philosophy' occurs only once in the New Testament (Colossians 2:8), and is used as a term of the same type as 'vain deceit' (p. 91).
as Richard Dawkins puts it: Professor Richard Dawkins, 'No mercy on the violent river of life', the *Daily Telegraph*, London, 10 May 1995.
Professor Dawkins... says nature is not cruel, only pitilessly indifferent: he comments, 'This is one of the hardest lessons for humans to learn. We cannot accept that things might be neither good nor evil, neither cruel nor kind, but simply indifferent to all suffering, lacking all purpose.'

Jesus... refers to the neutrality... of nature: Matt. 5:45.

foxes and birds are better housed than he is: Matt. 8:20; Luke 9:58.

God doesn't forget a single sparrow: Matt. 10:29; Luke 12:6.

wolves: in Matt. 10:16 (also Luke 10:3) Jesus tells his disciples that he is sending them out like sheep in the midst of wolves.

poisonous snakes and scorpions: Luke 10:19, where Jesus tells his disciples that he has given them power to tread on snakes and scorpions.

earthquakes as symptoms of this world's destruction: Mark 13:8; Matt. 24:7; Luke 21:11.

He also talks of floods and of a river bursting its banks: Luke 6:48; cf. Matt. 7:25-27 which also mentions gales.

walking on water: Mark 6:48-51; Matt. 14:25; John 6:19-21.

feeding five thousand men: Mark 6:35-44; Matt. 14:15-21; Luke 9:12-17; John 6:5-13.

an unspecified number of women and children: Matt. 14:21 (they are not mentioned by the other Gospel writers).

convenient to treat them as a separate category from Jesus' healing miracles: see, for example, John Macquarrie, *Jesus Christ in Modern Thought*, London, SCM Press, 1990, pp. 79 ff.

we have to ask whether John... intended such a story to be taken literally: Macquarrie, p. 120.

not the power to change water into wine, but to give eternal life: John C. Fenton, *Finding the Way through John*, London, Mowbray, 1988, p. 17.

we're told by a Greek writer in the century before Jesus: *Diodorus Siculus* iii. 66. 2.

Pliny tells a similar story in his *Natural History*, ii. 231.

the miracle of Jesus walking on the Sea of Galilee: Mark 6:47-51; Matt. 14:25-26; John 6:19. This is the only miracle that is not reported by Luke, but is reported by John.

Mark's Gospel has been particularly singled out: so Rudolf Bultmann, *The History of the Synoptic Tradition*, Harper & Row and Blackwell, 1963, p. 241.

one of the most striking stories of this kind is told by Matthew: Matt. 17:24-27.

several parallels to this story: *The New Jerusalem Bible*, p. 1639, note j to Matt. 17.

a story... Herodotus tells: *Herodotus* iii. 40-43.

he even compares himself to a hen: Matt. 23:37; Luke 13:34.

a remark in one of Mishima's novels: Yukio Mishima, *The Temple of Dawn*, translated from the Japanese by E. Dale Saunders and Cecilia Segawa Seigle, Harmondsworth, Penguin Books, 1977, p. 22.